GWEN JOHN

I0418972

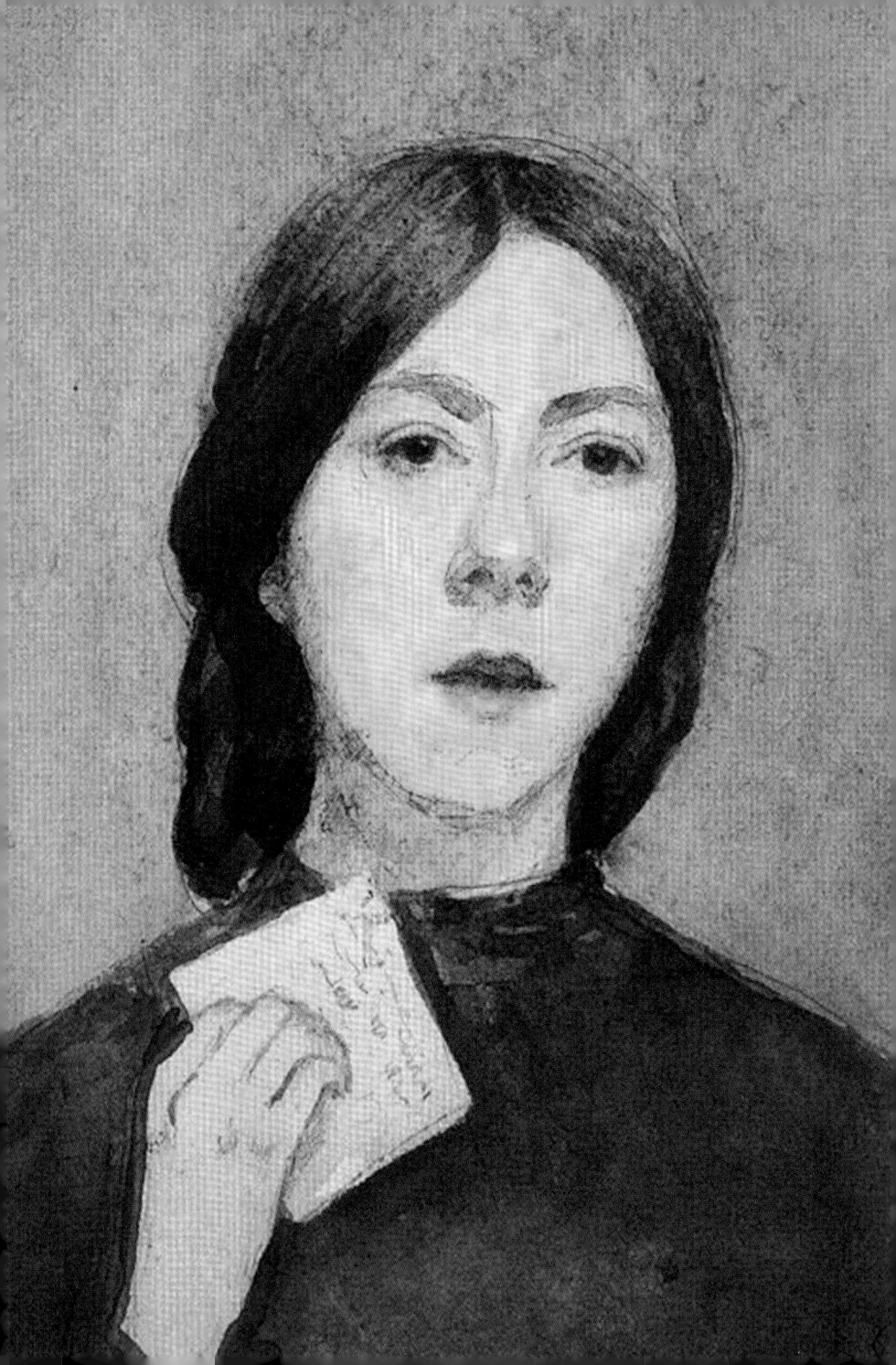

GWEN JOHN

EMMA CHAMBERS

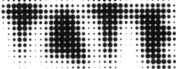

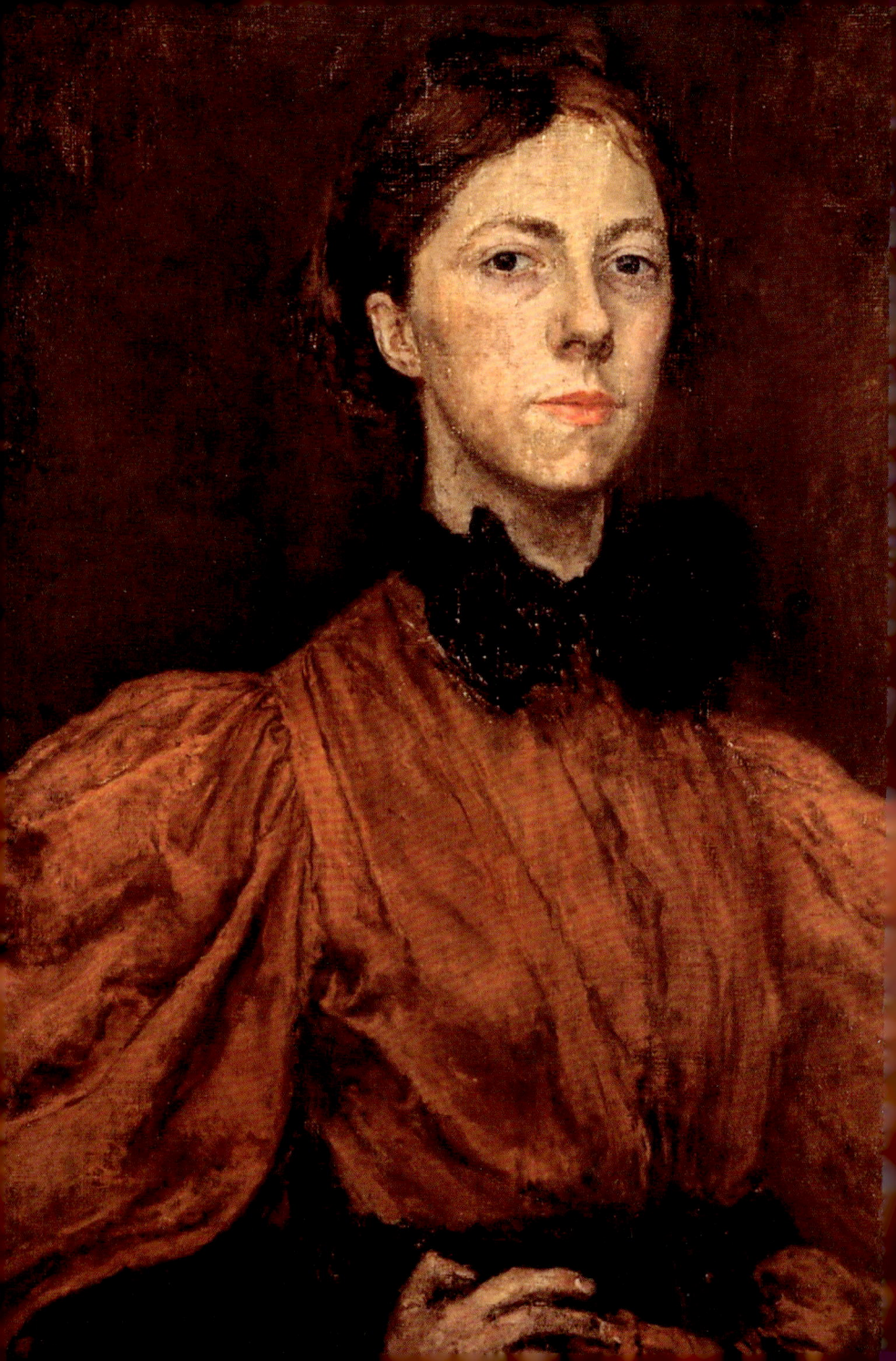

Gwen John is known for her subtle depictions of women in interior spaces, painted with a muted palette. Yet within these apparently serene works, an intense artistic engagement with the subjects was in play. As one sitter described, 'I feel the absorption of her personality as I sit.'[1] Writing about her later work, John described her approach to painting as an 'affair of volumes' where the subject was of less importance than the understanding of forms in space.[2] She honed these investigations of form through the execution of series of similar works in which the same motif was repeatedly reworked, and documented her meticulous investigation of colour, composition and technique in her notes on painting tones and methods.

John's often-quoted desire for 'an interior life', and her subject matter, led early commentators on her work to consider her as an artist working in isolation.[3] Far from being reclusive, however, she exhibited her works in both Paris and London and they were highly regarded by critics, collectors and her fellow artists.

She began her career with an emphatic public statement of artistic identity: a confident self-portrait, painted in London in 1899 and exhibited at the New English Art Club (NEAC) in 1900 (opposite). In this first public presentation of her work John defined herself as an artist in the swaggering, flamboyant tradition of the old masters, possibly basing the pose on a Rembrandt self-portrait in the National Gallery.[4] As Alicia Foster has argued, the painting was also important in the statement it made about the position of women in the art world: at a time when women were arguing for political enfranchisement and greater social freedom, John depicted herself wearing the practical separate blouse and skirt of the contemporary 'New Woman', and the work made an emphatic statement about the new status claimed by women in early twentieth-century society.[5]

In around 1902 John painted another self-portrait, which has become a defining image of the increased presence and confidence of women in the twentieth-century art world (p.6).[6] This time she set aside the references to the work of male old master artists and painted herself in the precise, pared-down style that would become the hallmark of her early work. John's steady gaze and expression of quiet determination communicate her desire to establish herself as an artist on her

Self Portrait 1899
Oil paint on canvas
61 × 37.8

5

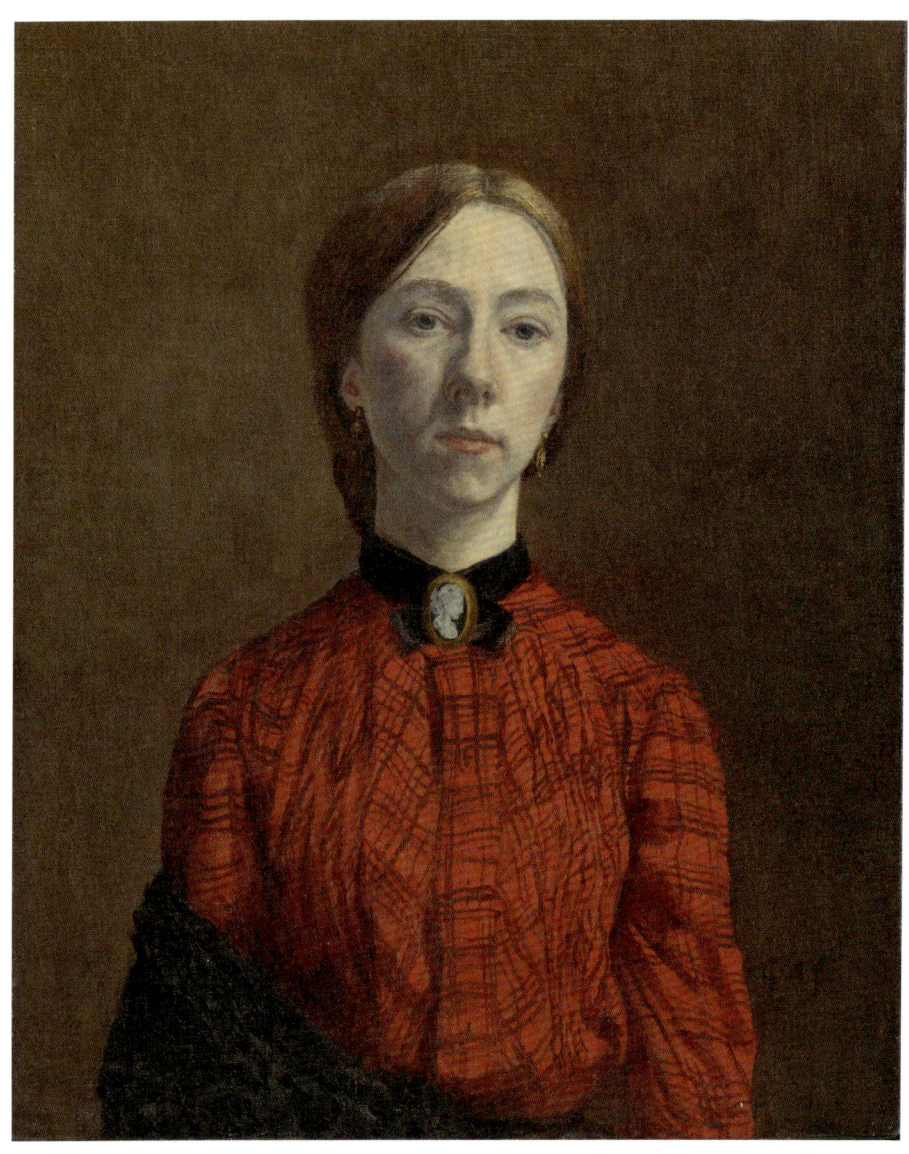

Self Portrait in a Red Blouse
c.1902
Oil paint on canvas
44.8 × 34.9

own terms. The work was shown at a 1902 exhibition of past and present students at the Slade School of Fine Art, where it was bought by Frederick Brown, Slade Professor during John's time there. His admiration for John as an artist – and for this painting in particular – is clear from his inclusion of her work in the background of his own self-portrait of 1926 (opposite).[7]

With these two self-portraits, John had made an immediate impact on the British art world, and she continued exhibiting regularly in London until 1911. Being a British artist based in France, however, gave her an independence from the groupings of modern artists who were her contemporaries in London and Paris. David Fraser Jenkins, Cecily Langdale and Alicia Foster have carefully traced the links between John's work and that of the French 'intimiste' painters in France and the Camden Town Group in London. Her work does indeed share some of the subject matter and handling of artists such as Walter Sickert, Harold Gilman and Spencer Gore who, like John, were influenced by James McNeill Whistler, Edgar Degas, Edouard Vuillard and Pierre Bonnard.[8] Yet, working independently, John developed a distinctive approach to her

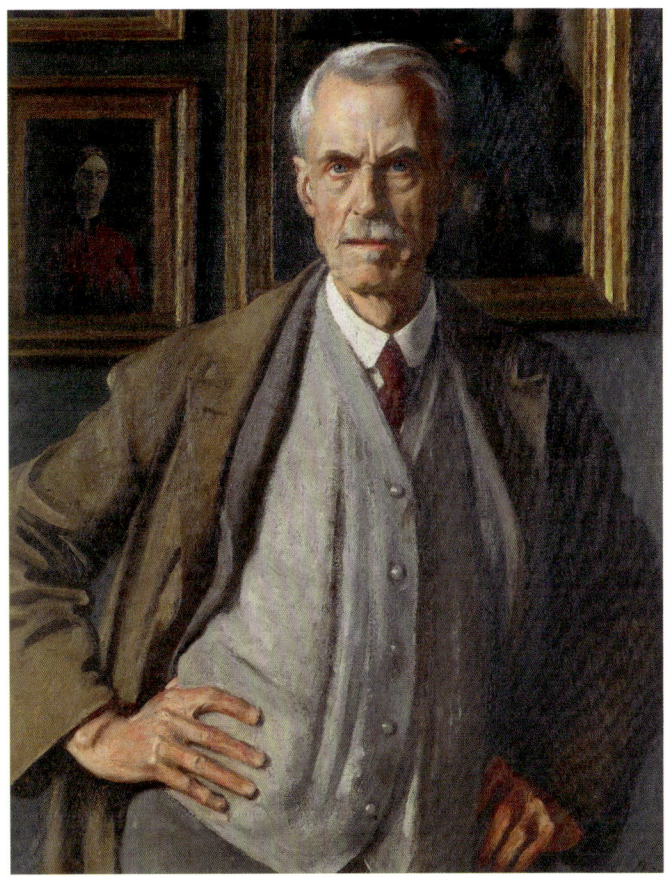

Frederick Brown
Portrait of the Artist 1926
Oil paint on canvas
97.5 × 68

subject matter. This was deliberately restricted to female figures in sparsely furnished interiors and avoided narrative content. John's simple compositions and muted range of tones were repeatedly refined to create a pictorial essence of quiet introspection.

However, it would be a mistake to create an equivalence between John's work and her life. In life she oscillated between a desire for solitude, in order to concentrate on her work, and intense passionate relationships with both men and women which profoundly disrupted her equilibrium. The mere fact of her living and working alone as a woman artist in Paris demonstrates John's determination to forge an independent existence in a way that was unusual for her contemporaries, and the high regard in which her work was held by fellow artists and collectors throughout her life shows that she did not overestimate her future status in the art world with these first two emphatic personal statements in self-portraiture. In 1910 she wrote to her friend Ursula Tyrwhitt: 'As to me I cannot imagine why my vision will have some value in the world – and yet I know it will … I think it will count because I am patient and *recueillie* in some degree.'[9] The French word *recueillie*, meaning calm and collected, is one that John used several times in her letters and sums up the serene intro-spection that her figures often convey to the viewer. It was a state of mind that she strove to attain herself – although she was often frustrated in achieving it.

THE SLADE

Gwen John was born in Haverfordwest, Pembrokeshire, in Wales, the daughter of Edwin John, a solicitor, and Augusta John, an amateur painter. John and her younger brother Augustus showed early artistic talent and both attended the Slade School of Fine Art in London (Augustus from 1894 and Gwen from 1895).

John was part of a cohort of talented students who studied at the Slade in the late 1890s, among them her friends Edna Waugh, Grilda Boughton-Leigh, Ursula Tyrwhitt, Ida Nettleship and Gwen Salmond. Other Slade contemporaries were William Orpen and Ambrose McEvoy. The Slade had been set up in 1871 as a more modern alternative to the Royal Academy; its curriculum was influenced by the French system of art education and, unlike the Royal Academy, from its foundation it had allowed female students to study from

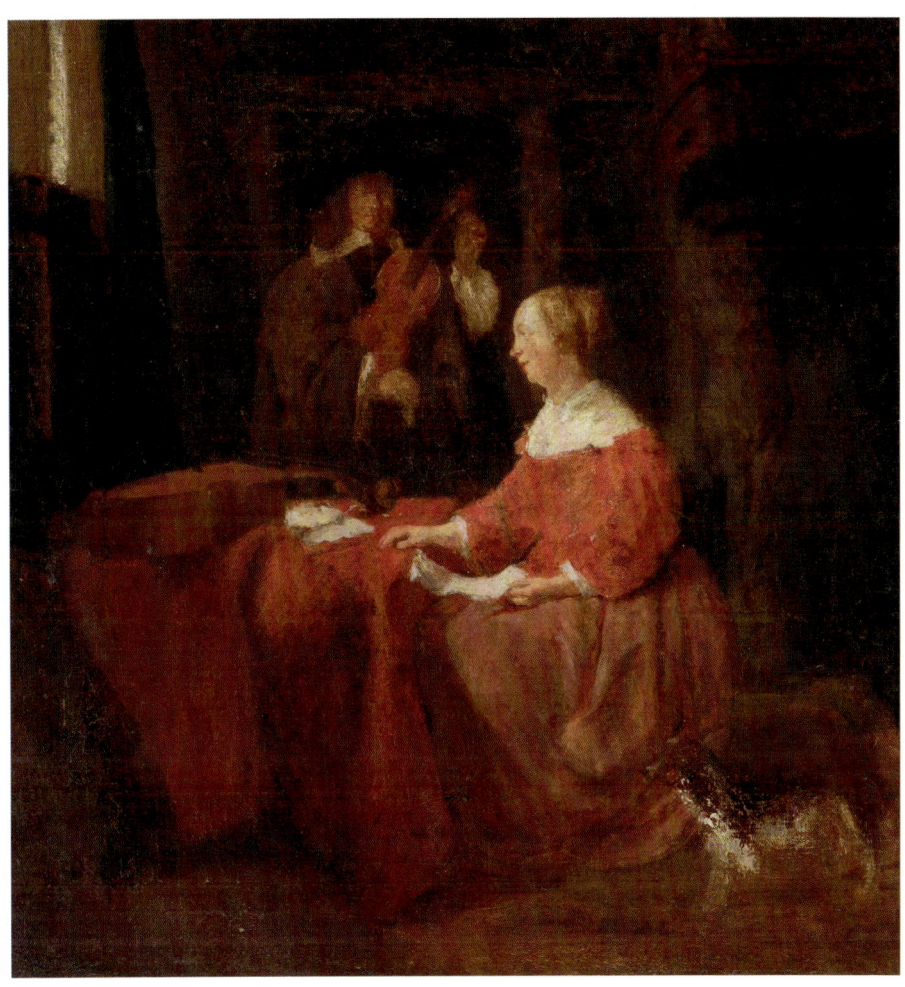

Copy after 'Woman Seated at a Table and a Man Tuning a Violin by Gabriel Metsu'
c.1896–8
Oil paint on canvas
41.9 × 36.8

the life model. In the 1890s, when John studied at the Slade, Frederick Brown was Slade Professor; other tutors included Henry Tonks – who taught a rigorous system of linear drawing based on Renaissance masters such as Michelangelo – and Philip Wilson Steer, who taught painting and whose own work was influenced by the French impressionists. Alongside their work in the Slade life rooms, students were encouraged to copy the paintings and drawings of the old masters in London museums. The only copy of a painting by another artist that John ever made was during her time at the Slade, when she produced a version of Gabriel Metsu's *Woman Seated at a Table* and a Man Tuning a Violin c.1658 (p.9), demonstrating an early interest in figures in interiors which was to dominate her subject matter throughout her career.

Another important contemporary figure for Slade students was James McNeill Whistler, whose restricted palette and tonal system of painting was highly influential on John's early work.[10] In 1898 John painted a portrait of her younger sister Winifred which, as Cecily Langdale has noted, demonstrates John's admiration for Whistler's work, both in its pose and in the use of a subdued range of tones enlivened by a single

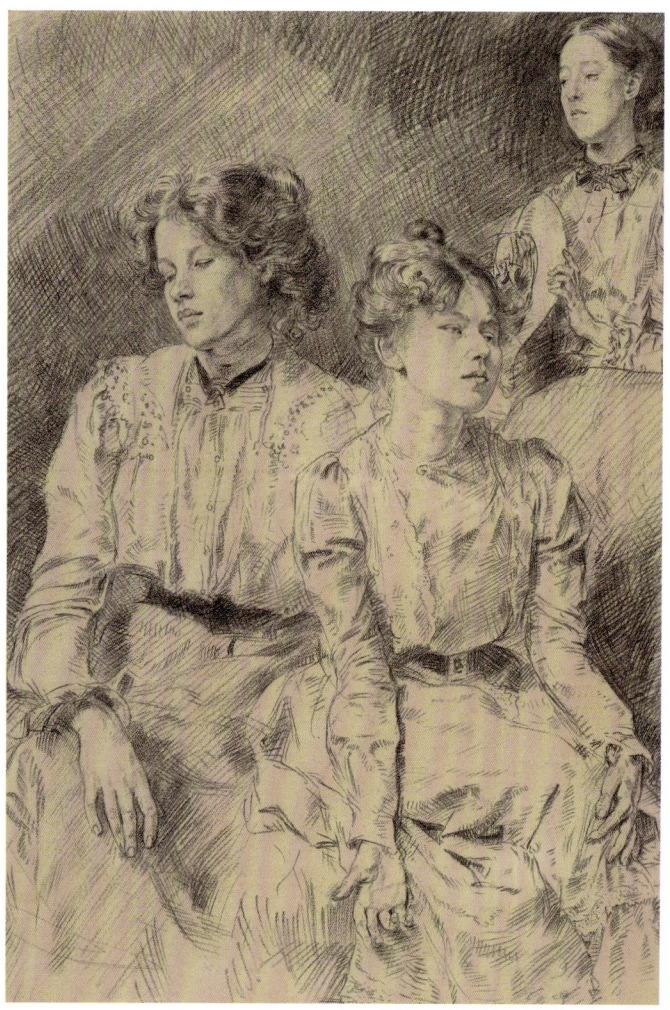

Augustus John
Gwen John, Ida Nettleship and Ursula Tyrwhitt c.1898–9
Black chalk on paper
33 × 25.1

splash of colour: the sitter's red scarf (p.33).[11] *Portrait of Mrs Atkinson*, painted around the same time, also uses a limited range of earth colours applied in thin layers with fine brushes so that no brushstrokes are visible (pp.34–5).[12] Here, John places the sitter in a contemporary interior, and the framed pictures on the wall, juxtaposed with the dark mass of the sitter's dress and the fine rendering of her features, evoke Whistler's portrait of his mother *Arrangement in Grey and Black No.1* 1871. It is likely that the interior depicted is the lodgings at 21 Fitzroy Street that John shared with her brother in 1897–8, which also forms the background to the *Portrait Group* 1897–8, in which John portrayed her siblings Augustus and Winifred with fellow Slade students Rosa Waugh and Michel Salaman (pp.30–1). This watercolour captures the unconventional social milieu of the Slade, where men and women mixed freely and where John formed many of her lasting friendships. Augustus drew John together with her Slade school friends Ida Nettleship and Ursula Tyrwhitt in c.1898–9 (opposite). These school connections were to continue into later life, with Ida marrying Augustus and Ursula becoming a lifelong friend with whom John corresponded all her life.

STUDYING IN PARIS

After leaving the Slade, John moved to Paris in autumn 1898 to study at the Académie Carmen with Whistler. Here she shared lodgings with Ida Nettleship and Gwen Salmond, and Ida's letters to her mother from that time give a flavour of the women's lives as they used each other as models and planned future compositions. Ida wrote: 'Gwen s. and J. are painting me, and we are all 3 painting Gwen John'; and 'Gwen John is sitting before a mirror carefully posing herself. She has been at it for half an hour. It is for an "interior".'[13] The only painting by John known to survive from this time is *The Friends* c.1898–9, in which Nettleship and Salmond pose for 'an interior' in their Paris rooms at 12 Rue Froidevaux (p.32).

Even at this early stage of her career John was already establishing the subject matter of female sitters in domestic interiors that would dominate her work in later years. This was not unusual for the time, given the influence of Whistler and seventeenth-century Dutch painters such as Johannes Vermeer on John's contemporaries. Former Slade students such as Orpen and William Rothenstein pioneered the genre of the 'portrait interior' in the early 1900s, with Rothenstein

William Orpen
The Mirror 1900
Oil paint on canvas
50.8 × 40.6

The Student 1903–4
Oil paint on canvas
56.1 × 33.1

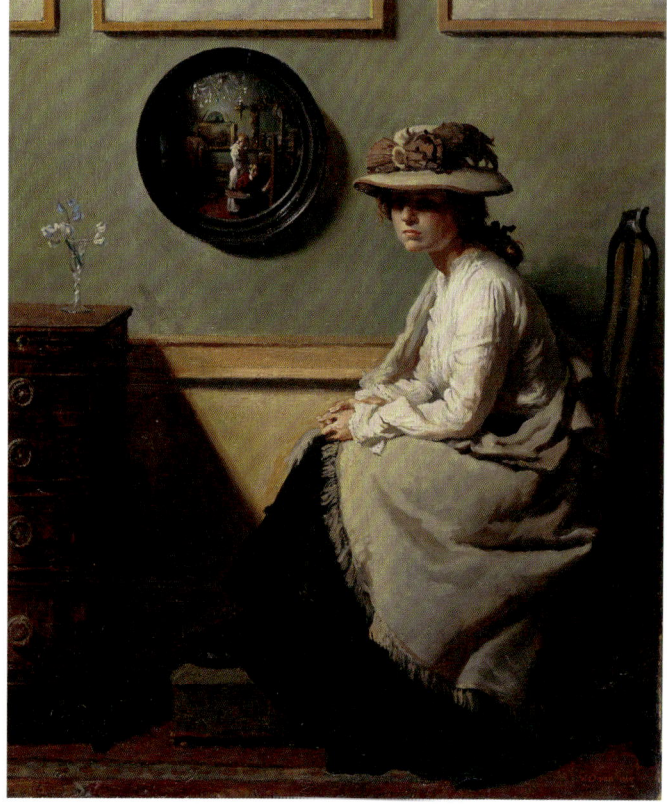

later recalling that what he called 'small "interior" subjects'
were a distinctive group of works that he began in 1900.[14]
Rothenstein's *The Browning Readers* 1900 and Orpen's *The Mirror*
1900 (above) are key examples of this genre, which often
featured in NEAC exhibitions in the 1900s.

WALKING TO TOULOUSE

Far from living the restricted, interior existence which her
choice of subject matter might imply, John was an adventurous
artist who was determined to experience life free of the
constraints usually imposed on women in the early twentieth
century. In summer 1903 she embarked on a walking tour
across France with her friend Dorothy McNeill (nicknamed
Dorelia). The pair intended to travel from Bordeaux to Rome,
earning money by selling sketches, but only got as far as
Toulouse, where they spent the winter. Here, John painted
several portraits of Dorelia, two of them showing the sitter

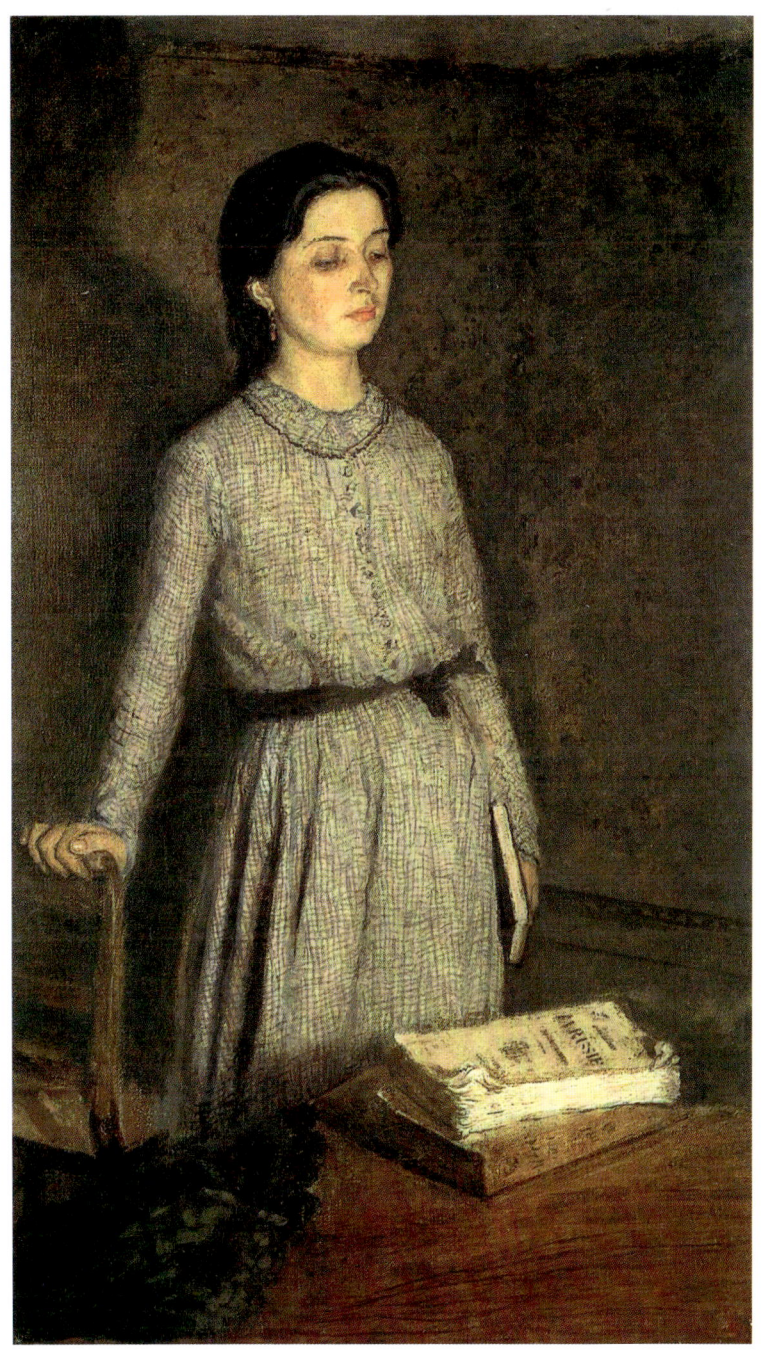

as an introspective figure in a lamplit room studiously absorbed in her books. *The Student* 1903–4 (p.13) exemplifies the simple elements which John would use to create her compositions throughout her life: the subtle tonalities of the palette, the play of light and the self-absorption and introspection of the sitter in a sparse interior.[15]

Returning to Paris from Toulouse in spring 1904, John established herself in the capital. She had a small regular income from her mother's estate, and took up modelling, mainly for female artists, to support herself.[16] In 1904 she began modelling for Rodin, writing to Tyrwhitt that she was sitting for him every day and he had begun a statue – she was posing as the *Muse* for his *Monument to Whistler*.[17] John's relationship with Rodin – which was sexually and emotionally intense, and took up much of her time and energy – can be traced by the numerous letters John wrote to him that survive in the archive of the Musée Rodin.[18] Heavily invested in this new relationship, her focus moved to modelling for Rodin rather than making her own work; she made very few paintings, but many drawings, which she would take to Rodin for his comments. These drawings included figure studies and several depicting her cats, influenced by Rodin's linear and fluid style of drawing (pp.38–41).[19]

In 1906, John began a new series of works in which interior settings appeared as a more prominent part of the composition. Having moved to a room on Rue St Placide, she wrote to Rodin about her delight in her new surroundings: 'My room is lovely… I'm going to do some drawings or paintings to show you what I think is so pretty about it. I'm going to do some in the mirror of my wardrobe – with me as the figure occupied somehow with something … like the Dutch paintings in subject.'[20] The first of these paintings was *La Chambre sur la Cour* c.1907–8 (opposite), and the theme was later developed into a sequence of related paintings with a female figure reading at a window.

John also began to paint interiors without figures, where the objects in the painting suggest a simple life and evoke a recent human presence. *A Corner of the Artist's Room in Paris* 1907–9 (p.44), painted after she had relocated to 87 Rue Cherche-Midi in spring 1907, shows the cane chair and wooden table which appear in multiple works of this period, while the parasol and coat suggest that the artist has just arrived in the room.

These interiors, which draw on the familiar imagery of the artist's studio, seem to invite the viewer into John's world and offer tantalising clues to her life through the few simple objects which occupied her working environment.[21] Like her early self-portraits, these works are a statement of the independence afforded by her own studio space, and a reminder of its centrality to her work.

1907 was a pivotal year in John's life. It marked the death of her friend Ida Nettleship and the waning of her relationship with Rodin, which was now conducted mostly through correspondence, although she was still sitting for him.[22] The drawing *Autoportrait à la Lettre*, in which John portrays herself eagerly holding a letter, demonstrates the importance of this correspondence to her, and the drawing is one of several

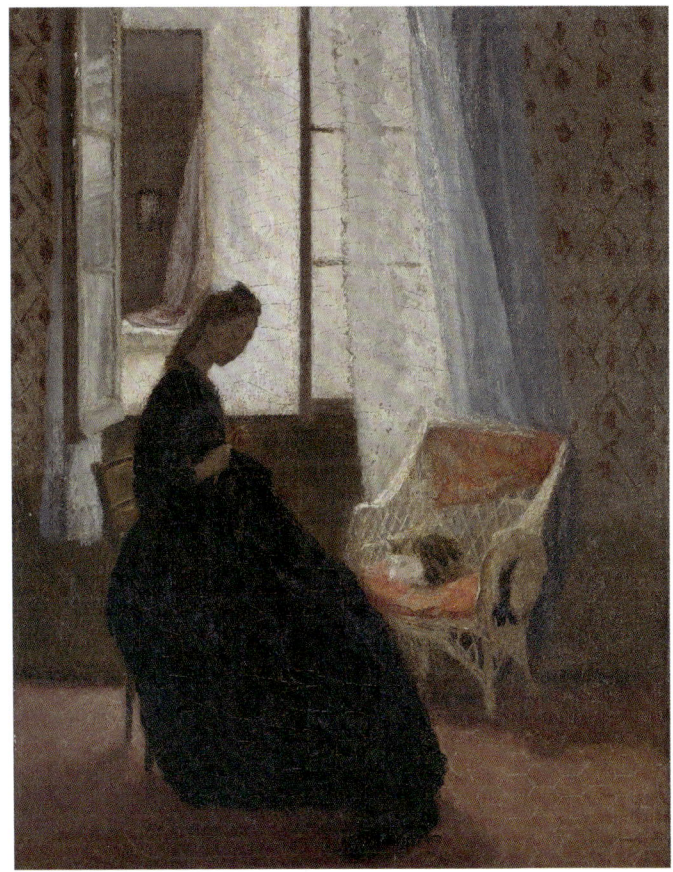

La Chambre sur la Cour
c.1907–8
Oil paint on canvas
31.8 × 21.6

that remained in Rodin's possession (pp.2, 37). In her new residence on Rue Cherche-Midi, she began a portrait of her friend Chloë Boughton-Leigh (p.42). Painted in sandy browns and light greys, this portrait shows the subtle gradations of tone that Gwen John had learned from Whistler and her ability to use the intimacy of the portrait sitting to connect with her subjects and capture their distinct personality. In 1908 she exhibited the portrait at the NEAC in London to critical acclaim, The Studio's reviewer writing: 'Miss Gwen John's pictures ... seek earnestly in the colour which ordinary life wears for lasting effects of beauty. Her portrait of Miss C. Boughton-Leigh seems to us one of the greatest achievements in this exhibition because of this sincerity.'[23]

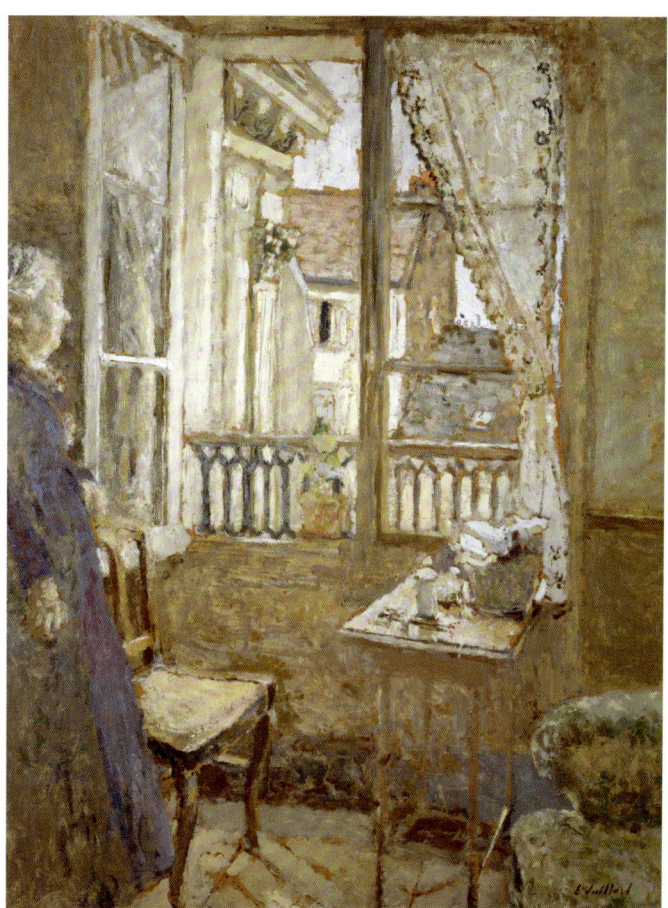

Edouard Vuillard
La Fenêtre Ouvert c.1902–3,
reworked 1915
Oil paint on board
56.9 × 45

In 1909 John moved to Rue de l'Ouest, Montparnasse. *A Lady Reading* c.1910–11 (p.46) places a figure in this new interior, which retains the cane chair and the table from Rue Cherche-Midi, adding a red checked curtain and a wall of framed pictures including John's own drawings of cats. Although the room is John's own, filled with her possessions, the figure is not a self-portrait, and she wrote to Tyrwhitt that she had been inspired by Dürer's work when painting the features: 'I tried to make it look like a *vièrge* of Durer ... I did it because I didn't want to have my own face there.'[24] (In a later version of the composition, *Girl Reading at the Window* 1911 (p.47), John replaced the face of the reading girl with a self-portrait).[25] As well as the echo of Dürer's Madonnas in the figure's facial features, the composition of *A Lady Reading* draws on conventions of the Annunciation in Northern Renaissance religious painting, in which a female figure reading by a window was frequently used to signify the Virgin Mary. Although inspired by Dutch interiors, John uses objects associated with Parisian artists' studios such as the wicker chair and red checked curtain to create a contemporary interior.[26] Additionally, the work echoes Vuillard's 'intimiste' paintings depicting female figures in domestic spaces, such as *La Fenêtre Ouvert* c.1902–3, reworked 1915 (opposite).[27]

THE NUDE & THE CLOTHED FIGURE

In 1909 John began work on a pair of paintings depicting the model Fenella Lovell.[28] One painting showed the sitter clothed, the other undressed (pp.19, 48–9). The nude was a rare subject in John's art, but she was familiar with the role of life model, having sat for Rodin and other artists since 1904, and she also drew several nude self-portraits (p.18). Nude subjects in contemporary interiors were popularised by French painters such as Degas and Bonnard in the late nineteenth and early twentieth centuries as a way of connecting the genre with modern urban life; abandoning classical idealisation, these works located the nude within domestic spaces, engaged in intimate activities and unaware of being viewed, giving the viewer the illusion of access to a private world. John echoes these keyhole viewpoints in her drawing *Woman Dressing* c.1907 (p.50) which shows the figure in a modest contemporary interior similar to those seen in the works of Degas.

In Britain, artists such as Walter Sickert and Philip Wilson Steer were also painting nudes in contemporary interiors.

Self Portrait Nude c.1909
Graphite on paper
24.8 × 16.5

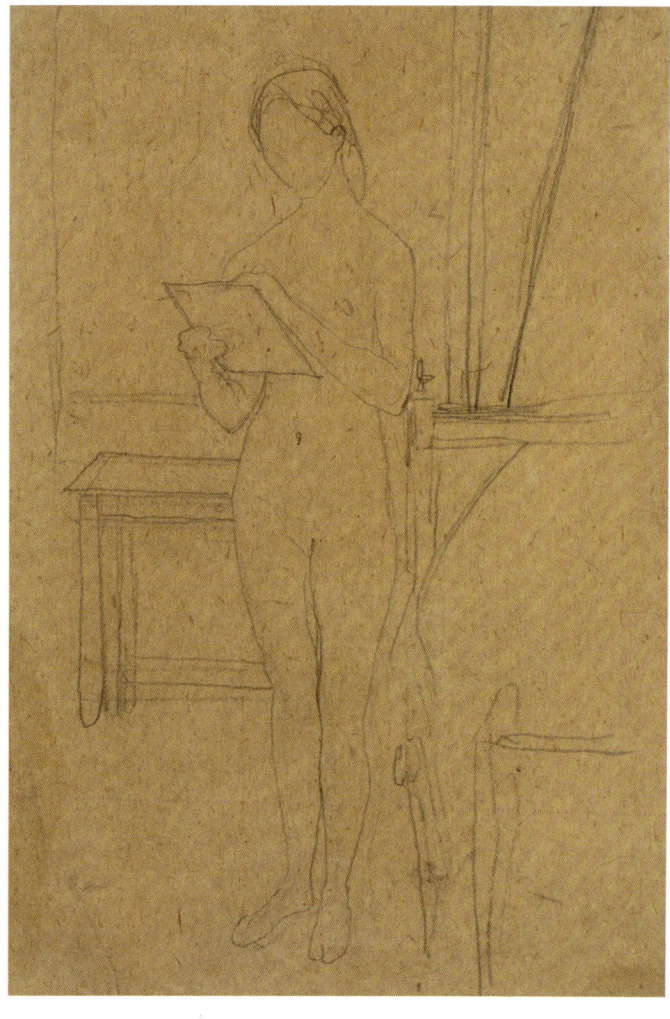

Sickert's Camden Town nudes were criticised for their seedy settings, which suggested the world of prostitution, while Steer's work *Seated Nude: The Black Hat* – in which a model has removed her clothing and flirtatiously poses in a hat in a studio setting – was deemed immoral because of the juxtaposition of nudity and discarded clothing (p.20).[29] This criticism of Steer's painting demonstrates the difference between the idea of the 'nude' and the 'undressed' figure in this period, and John deliberately plays with this distinction both in the pairing of the clothed and nude portraits and in the discarded clothing in *Nude Girl*, in which the sitter's dress has settled around her hips, representing an interim stage between naked and clothed.[30]

Together, John's objective approach, the shallow picture plane, the lack of room setting and the engagement with the sitter give *Nude Girl* a quality of intimacy that is not present in Steer's and Sickert's works. The vulnerability, weakness and fragility of the naked body is signalled through the specific thin, round-shouldered body type of the sitter and the rigidity

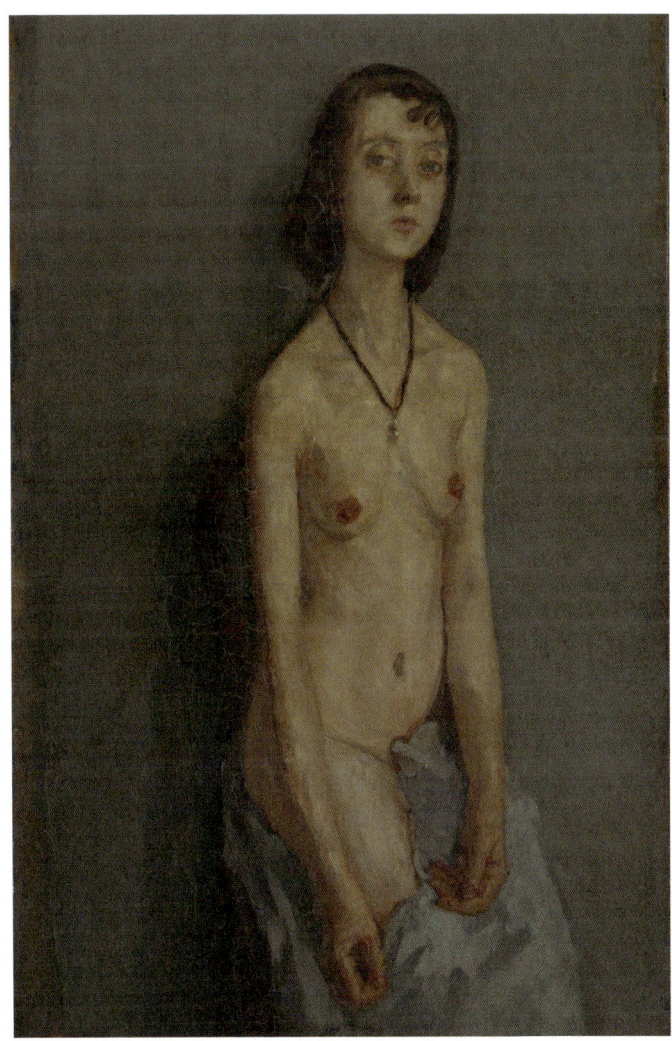

Nude Girl 1909–10
Oil paint on canvas
44.5 × 27.9

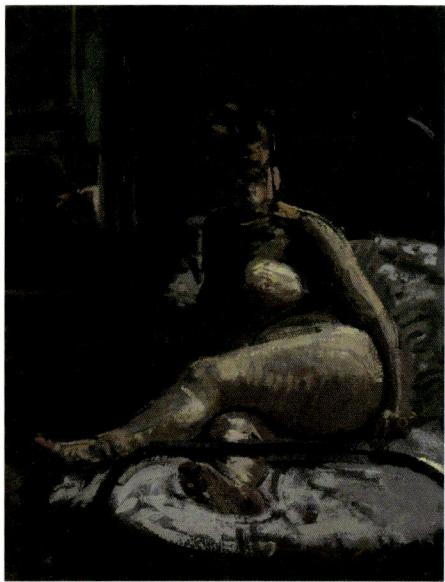

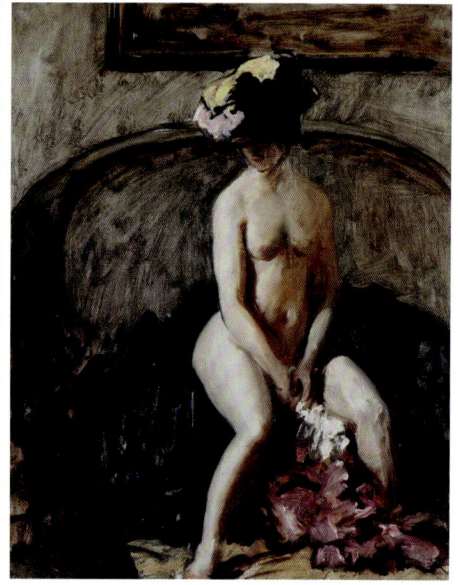

of her unusual pose, halfway between sitting and standing. The model's gaze reveals her awareness of the artist's presence and draws attention to the uncomfortable interaction between painter and model. John disliked Lovell, writing to Tyrwhitt: 'It is a great strain doing Fenella. It is a pretty little face but she is dreadful.'[31] This reminds us how intense and intimate the encounter between painter and model in a small studio space might be, and how this might shape the appearance of the work. It is clear that the pairing of clothed and naked portraits of the same sitter continued to interest John, who would return to the subject in 1923 (pp.82–3).

In 1910, Augustus introduced John to the American collector John Quinn, who became an important patron of her art. He first bought a picture of hers – *Girl Reading at the Window* (p.47) – in 1911, and from January 1913 he gave her payments in advance in return for having first choice of the work she produced.[32] Quinn's financial support was crucial in allowing John to concentrate on her art, and he formed a significant collection of her work before his death in 1924.[33] He was also responsible for publicising John's work in America, in 1913 lending *Girl Reading at the Window* to the *International Exhibition of Modern Art* in New York, known as the *Armory Show* – an important international survey of modern art.

Walter Sickert
La Hollandaise c.1906
Oil paint on canvas
51.1 × 40.6

Philip Wilson Steer
Seated Nude: The Black Hat
c.1900
Oil paint on canvas
50.8 × 40.6

PAINTING SERIES

In 1911 John moved to Rue Terre Neuve in Meudon, a suburb of Paris, travelling into the centre of the capital each day to work in her room on Rue de l'Ouest. This move brought her physically closer to Rodin, who also lived in Meudon (but spent most of his time at his studio in Paris) and, although she was still modelling for him occasionally, their relationship was floundering.[34] Meanwhile, John integrated herself into the small community of Meudon and began to attend church there, being received into the Catholic faith early in 1913. John's Catholic faith had an immediate impact on her work, and in 1913 she began a series of paintings of Mère Poussepin, the founder of the Dominican Sisters of Charity who had a convent in Meudon (p.52). These paintings, based on a printed prayer card, also marked the beginning of John's work in extended series. In 1916

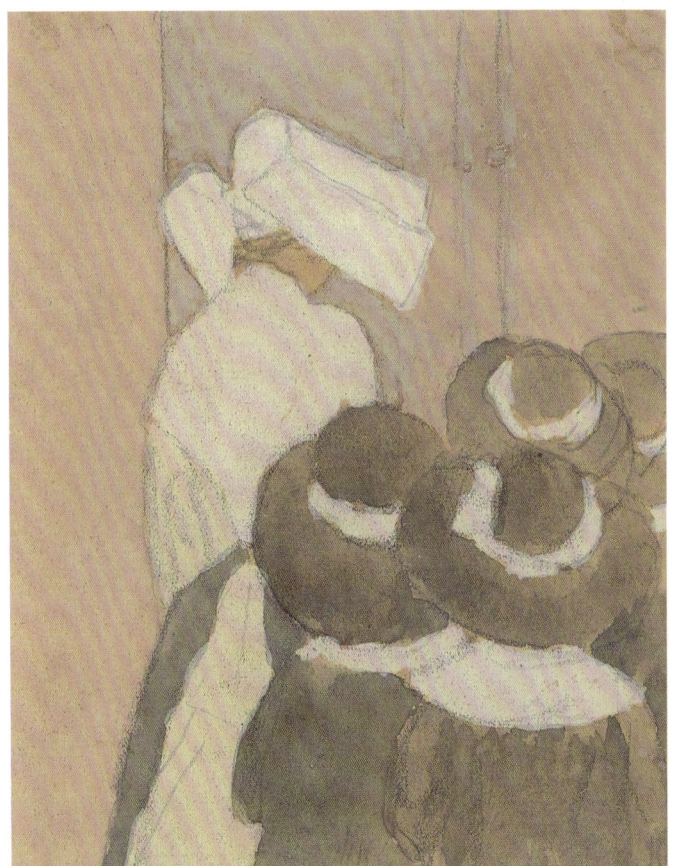

Nun with a Group of Orphans
c.1910
Watercolour, gouache and graphite on paper
15.9 × 12.4

she wrote to Tyrwhitt: 'I think a portrait ought to be done in 1 sitting or at most 2. For that one must paint a lot of canvases probably and waste them.'[35] This new approach to painting governs the many series of works in John's oeuvre that repeat the same composition with slight variations as the artist worked to resolve the problems of composition and tone in each canvas. Portraits of nuns would occupy her intermittently for at least eight years; in 1916 she told Quinn that the convent wanted one for every room and she was trying to do them simultaneously.[36]

At the same time as she was painting the nuns, she was making drawings of little girls from the Orphelinat St Joseph as they attended church (p.21).[37] These began as quickly sketched observations of glimpsed moments, but John would rework the drawings in her studio, retracing them to obtain the simple but strong line she required and adding watercolour washes. She described her method to Tyrwhitt: 'I first draw in the thing then trace it onto a clean piece of paper by holding it against the window. Then decide absolutely on the tones, then try to make them in colour and put them on flat ... I want my drawings ... to be definite and clean like Japanese drawings.'[38]

John's work was little changed by the outbreak of the First World War in 1914, although several of her letters to Tyrwhitt relate to her anxiety about bombings and the outcome of the war.[39] She remained in Paris and Meudon throughout, working on her paintings of nuns and beginning a sequence of paintings of a girl in a blue dress (p.54). The only hints of the war in her work were sketches of soldiers, and a series of pencil and wash portraits of French generals, painted from photographic source material.[40]

Two significant events occurred in 1917, towards the end of the war: the Contemporary Art Society presented John's paintings Nude Girl and A Lady Reading to Tate, making these the first of her works to enter a public collection, and then, that November, Rodin died, bringing to an end the most important relationship of her life.

In August 1918 and January 1919 John visited Pléneuf, a village on Brittany's north coast, where she made a series of drawings of local children (pp.55, 57). One of her regular sitters was Marie Hamonet, whom she called 'Annabella' (opposite). John exhibited nine drawings of Breton children at the Salon d'Automne in Paris in 1919, and in 1920 showed

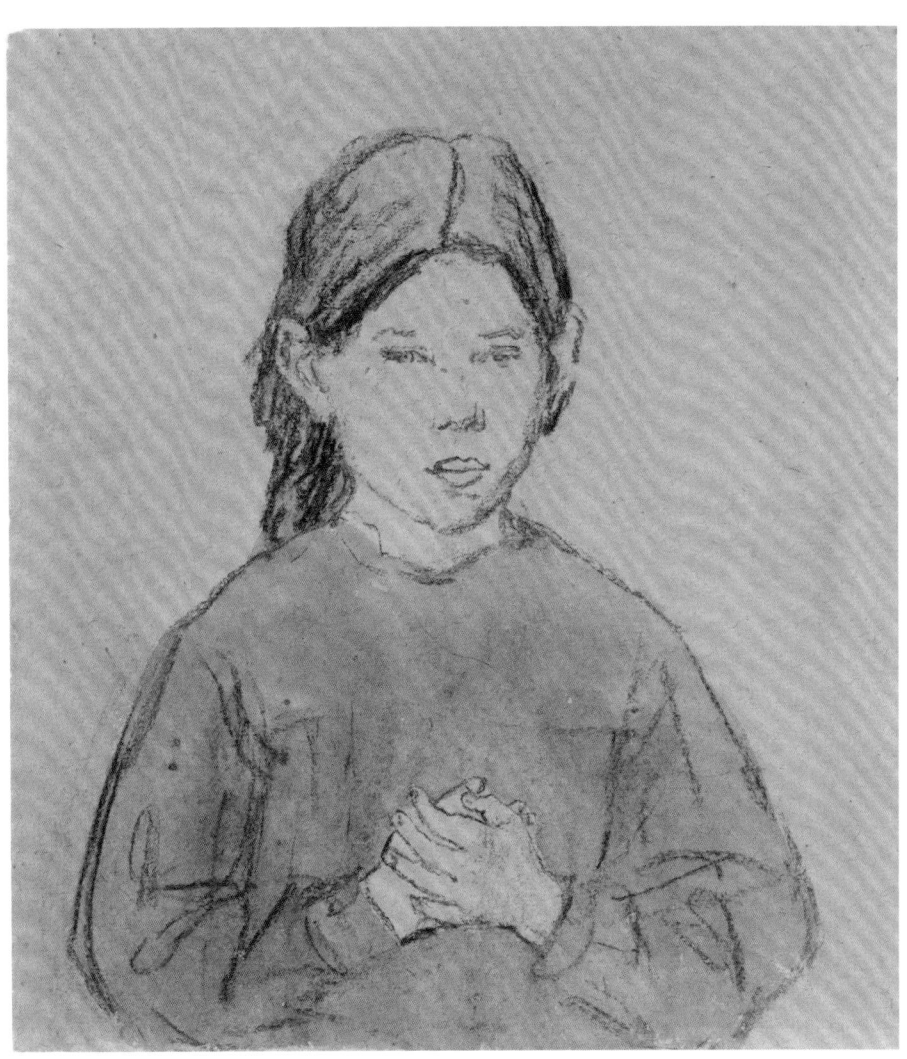

Annabella c.1915–20
Charcoal and watercolour
on paper
23.8 × 21

thirteen drawings at two different Paris salons, selling nearly all of them. Brittany represented a period of liberation for John away from Paris, and here she felt she had made great advances in her art through drawing rather than painting. Freed from the anxiety of her relationship with Rodin, and invigorated by her trips to Pléneuf, she increased her rate of production and on her return to Paris she continued to make many drawings of children, as well as several paintings, among them *Girl in Rose* in the early 1920s (p.58) and *La Petite Modèle* in the late 1910s (p.60).

NEW TECHNIQUES

From around 1910 John had started to make fundamental changes to her painting technique. She moved away from using thin fluid layers of paint finished with a top layer of varnish to create a smooth glossy surface, and began instead to use thick chalky paint applied in short strokes that remained visible in the finished composition. According to painting conservator Mary Bustin, who has made close analysis of these later techniques, John began to prime her own canvases with a mixture of chalk and animal-skin glue, which produced a smooth white absorbent layer on which to paint. This surface retained minute bubbles, which were not filled by the paint as she applied it in quick dabs, and which remain visible as white specks or highlights in the paint layer. The mixing of a small

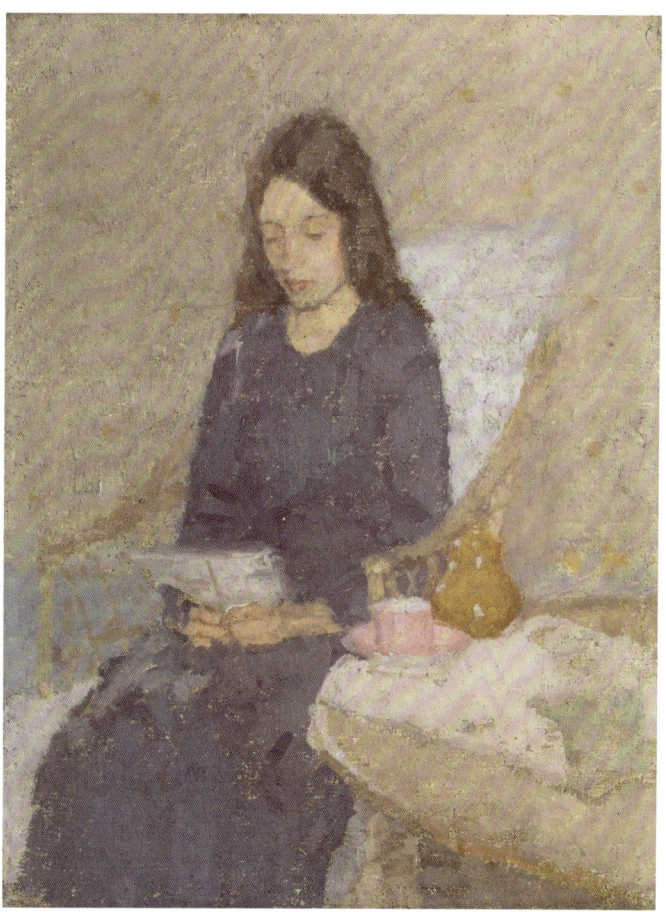

The Convalescent 1918–9
Oil paint on canvas
33.7 × 25.4

quantity of chalk with her colours made them into a thick paste that could be applied with precision.[41] She avoided using black for shading, instead using colour relationships to represent volumes and space, and mixed white pigment with her colours to achieve a reduced tonal range. When composing a work, John first made underdrawings on the primed canvas before applying her thickened paint in a mixture of short dabs and longer strokes. Rather than using outline to define the forms, she would stab the paint with dry bristles to soften the transitions between areas – a technique she called 'blobbing'.[42]

The paintings in the *Convalescent* series made between 1918 and 1924 show this new approach and use the cool palette and chalky opaque surfaces which were to characterise John's later work. *The Convalescent* shows a girl seated in a wicker chair alongside a table with teapot, cup and other items; she reads a letter, her eyes downcast to the page (opposite). John made ten versions of this composition (pp.61–5), and while the number of versions and their similarity reveal the artist at her most obsessively repetitive, there are subtle compositional changes from painting to painting in the girl's pose, her reading matter from letter to book, and the items on the table.

In these works John returns to the representation of a figure in an interior set back from the picture plane, rather than the representation of a figure against a simple background as seen in paintings of the earlier 1910s. As Cecily Langdale has noted, the paintings of the *Convalescent* series are related to John's interiors of 1907–9 in their focus on the interrelationships between objects and interior space.[43] Above all, they evoke an atmosphere of quiet, calm introspection, depicting a self-sufficient figure absorbed in an activity, unaware of the gaze of the viewer. Aside from the fact that she was a neighbour of John's in Meudon, nothing is known about the model for *The Convalescent*, although she appears in many of the artist's later paintings.[44]

MONUMENTAL FIGURES

In the 1920s John's work moved away from the specific interiors and small-scale figures of the *Convalescent* series, her figures becoming more monumental and their settings more abstracted and geometric. Although she painted a few still lifes (pp.68–77), her subject matter was now restricted to the depiction of three-quarter-length female figures, in sparse interiors often painted as a barely indicated backdrop (pp.78–81). The faces are painted in subtle naturalistic tones, while bodies are simplified into almost geometric forms, recalling the portraits of Cezanne and Picasso, but with a muted, restricted palette and a surface of textured dry paint applied with John's distinctive 'blobbing' brush technique.[45]

In 1922 John began working on a series of paintings with a new model, including *Girl with a Blue Scarf* c.1923–4 (p.84) and *Girl in a Mulberry Dress* c.1923–4 (p.85). The colour of the garment forms the focus of the composition in each case, occupying most of the picture plane (in contrast to the relatively small head and hands). In portraits such as *Girl Holding a Rose* early 1920s (opposite) and *The Pilgrim* c.1920 (p.78) the hands are enlarged and the figures are still more monumental.[46] John admired the work of Cezanne – once describing a book about him as 'very precious to her' – and Langdale notes a similarity between these paintings and Cezanne's late portraits with their massive immobile figures, small heads on large pyramidal bodies, and forceful brushstrokes.[47]

A decade later, in a letter to Ursula Tyrwhitt of 1936, John would describe her approach, in which the model was no longer an individual but a series of shapes requiring a pictorial solution: 'A cat & man it's the same thing … it's an *affaire of volumes*.'[48] In April 1921 she had written an extended series of notes on form, tone and colour, describing her practice in a way that gives an insight into her deliberative and methodical process.[49] Her later notes on portraiture, though written in 1932, could equally apply to these 1920s works:

The making of the portrait:
1. The strange form.
2. The pose and proportions.
3. The atmosphere and notes, the tones.
4. The finding of the forms (the sphere – the hair, the forehead, the cheek, the eye, the nose, the mouth, the neck, the chin, *the torse*)[sic].
5. Blobbing.
6. The sculpting with the hands.[50]

The early 1920s were also a period of stability in John's personal life. She formed several significant friendships, including one with Quinn's friend Jeanne Robert Foster, who visited her in Meudon in September 1920.[51] Quinn himself increased

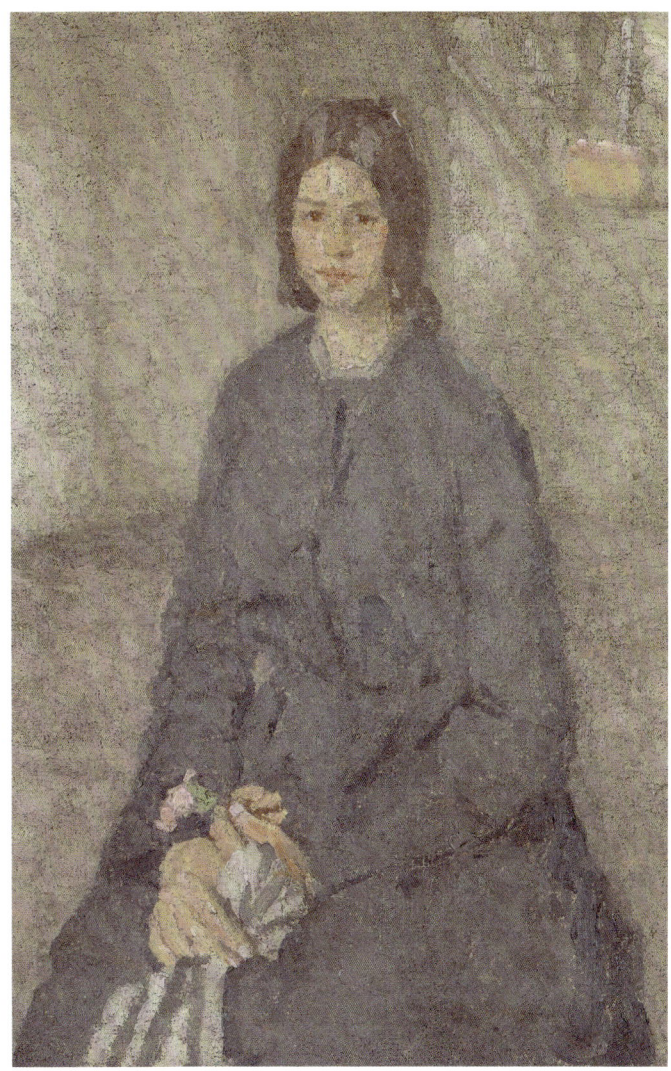

Girl Holding a Rose early
1920s
Oil paint on canvas
45.1 × 36.8

his support and he and John finally met in person in August
1921.[52] In these years, John exhibited regularly at the Paris
salons, showing work in 1920, 1923 and 1924, and her
comments on these exhibitions belie her image as a solitary
figure.[53] In 1924, for example, she wrote to Quinn: 'It is
amusing to have things in [the exhibition] and to go and see
them at the vernissage and to give vernissage cards to friends
and make rendez-vous!'[54] In March 1922 Quinn lent the five

paintings he owned to a show of British art, *Seven English Modernists*, at the Sculptors Gallery in New York, reporting to John that 'they were very much admired'.[55]

Quinn died suddenly in July 1924, leaving no provision for John in his will, resulting in considerable financial insecurity for her. Many of the works John was painting at that time had been intended for him, and this uncertainty affected her production.[56]

NEW CHENIL GALLERIES RETROSPECTIVE

In 1926 John re-engaged with the London art world, with a retrospective of her work at the New Chenil Galleries in London that ran from May to July. Her long absence from the London exhibition scene led to her being described as 'An Undiscovered Artist' in an article about the show in *Country Life*.[57] While the reviewer, Mary Chamot, compared John's work to that of Whistler, Degas and Vuillard, she stressed, too, that John could not be considered an impressionist because of the deliberation and monumental qualities of her work, whose atmosphere Chamot identified as most closely resembling the works of Vermeer: 'Like him, she prefers quiet scenes, mostly single figures in repose.' Chamot also remarked on the atmospheric effect of John's handling and palette: 'The last paintings are so light with such delicate contrasts, that they appear as through a haze, neither dull nor over-sunny, but just radiant with a quiet luminosity.'[58] The effect of seeing John's paintings en masse was also noted by her artist contemporaries: her fellow Slade student Michel Salaman, who had recently bought *The Pilgrim*, wrote: 'It was indeed a chastening joy to stand there amongst those pale, quiet songs of yours – like listening to the still music of the harpsichord – only there is nothing antique or archaic about your work. They are so intensely modern in all but their peacefulness.'[59]

THE LAST DECADE

John painted less after 1926, and her life was focused even more on the church. She began a friendship with Véra Oumançoff, which was similar in dynamic to her relationship with Rodin in its romantic intensity and letter-based conversation.[60] In 1929 John bought a plot of land with a building she used as a studio on Rue Babie in Meudon, taking pleasure in its garden as a home for her cats. Her last work in oils was a series of small paintings of a woman in a hat seated in profile in front of a window (pp.90–1). Six versions of this composition in oil and gouache painted in the 1930s show John's continued interest in developing the figure as a series of geometric forms.[61] Meanwhile, her health was worsening, and on 10 September 1939, during a visit to Dieppe, she collapsed in the street. She was taken to hospital where she died on 18 September.

It is likely that by travelling to Dieppe when she was already seriously ill, John was attempting to recapture the restorative effects that the coast had always had for her, particularly in Brittany. Looking back at her life, it is clear that although she spent the majority of her time making intensely focused paintings in her studio, the freedom of drawing by the sea and in church were equally important to her. While she painted little in her later years, many of her most detailed notes on paintings are from the 1930s and she evidently spent much of her time thinking about how to refine her compositions and techniques.

By this time, John had gained an institutional presence, with her paintings held in several museum collections including Tate, Manchester Art Gallery, Hugh Lane Gallery in Dublin, the Albright–Knox Gallery in Buffalo, New York and the Art Institute of Chicago. This public accessibility of her work brought increased recognition, and a memorial exhibition of her work was held at the Matthiesen Gallery in London in 1946. However, at the same time as this mid-twentieth-century period of public recognition, the persistent depiction of John's life as solitary and ascetic also took hold. Fortunately, this myth has been increasingly challenged by research on her art and life, which has revealed her engagement with art world networks and reinserted her into narratives of twentieth-century modern art, as she deserves.[62] We can now appreciate John's inner life and her public presence equally. As she wrote to Ursula Tyrwhitt in February 1909: 'I think that is a beautiful idea that we dig out the precious things hidden in us when we paint – and quite true.'[63]

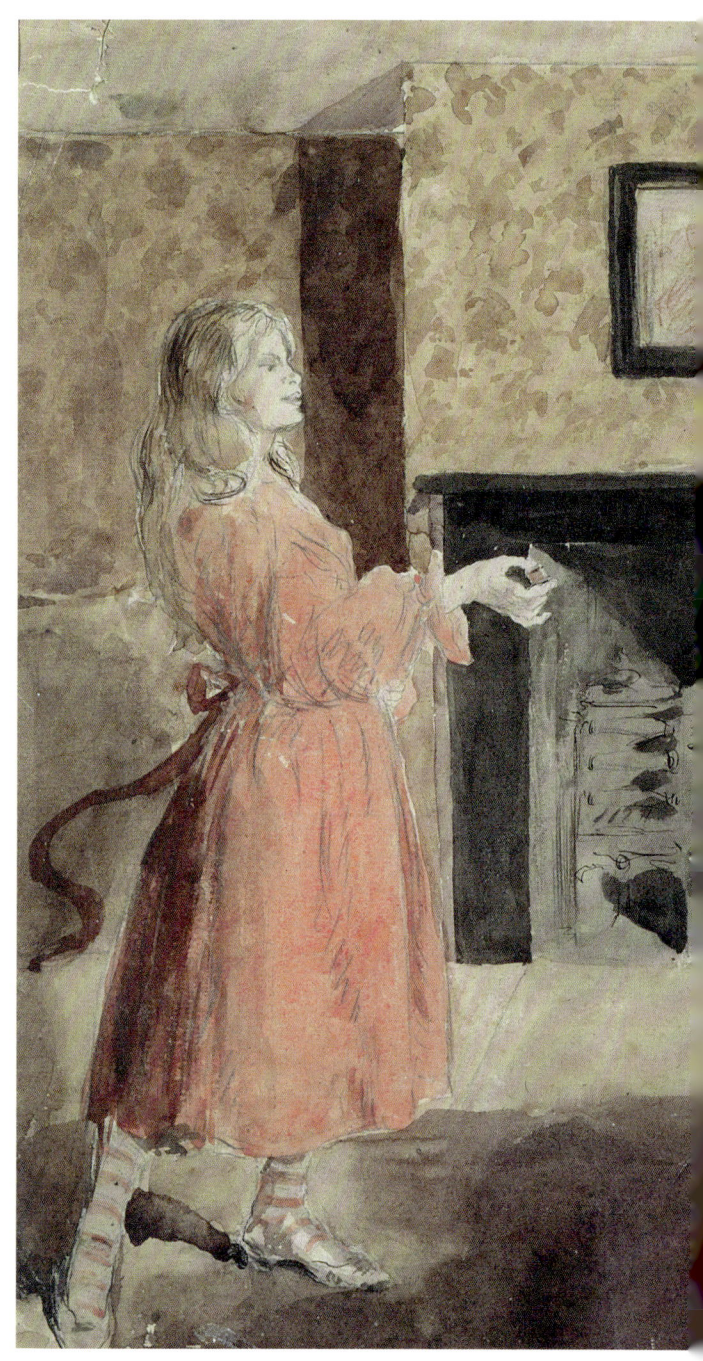

Portrait Group 1897–8
Pen and watercolour over
graphite on paper
27.9 × 38.1

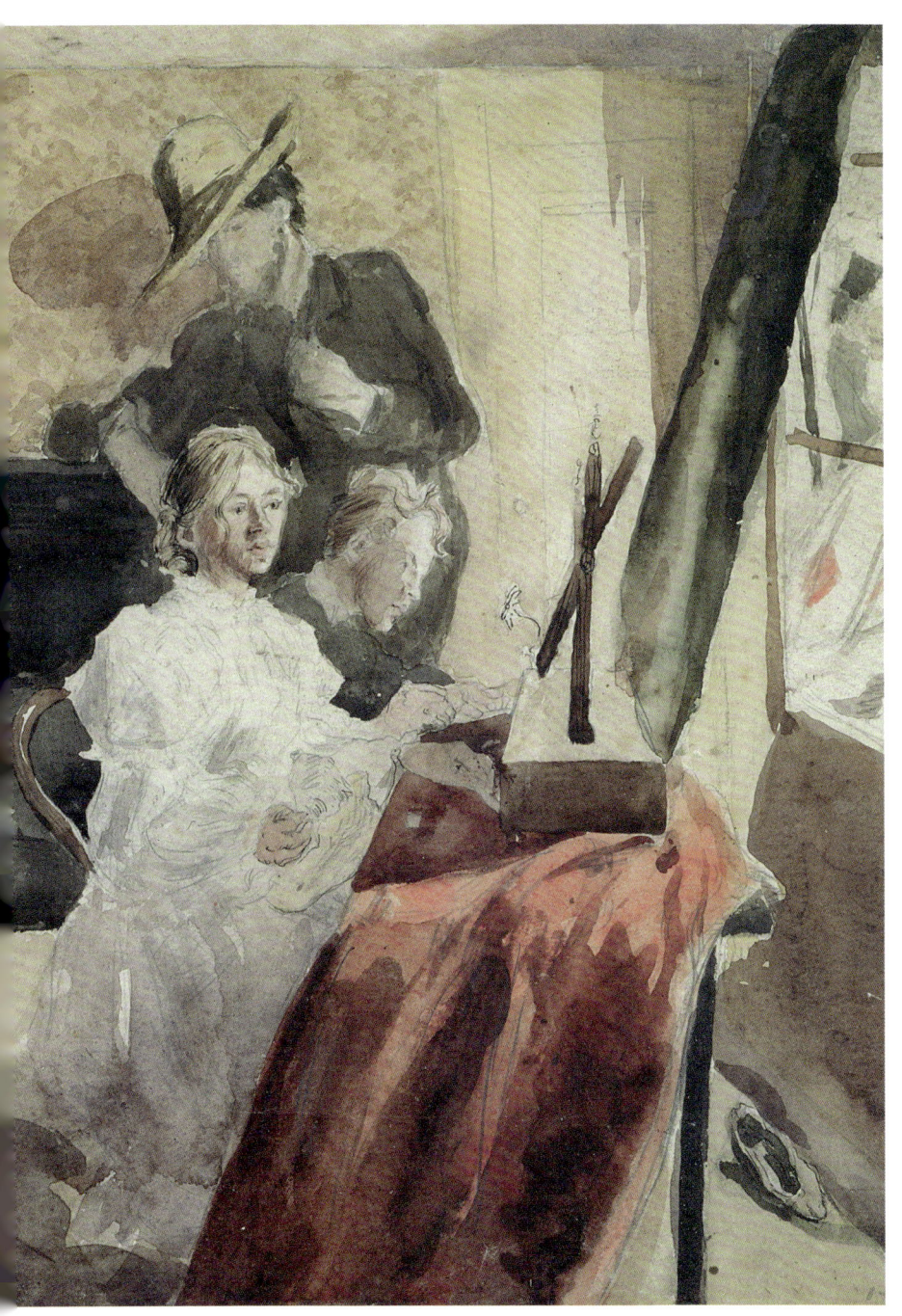

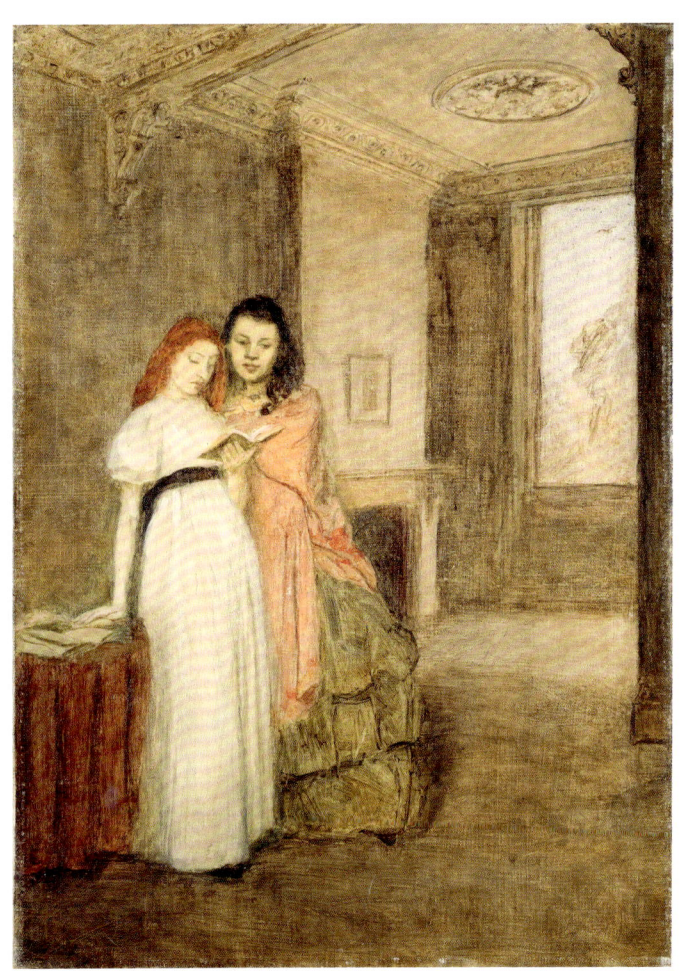

The Friends c.1898–9
Oil paint on canvas
46 × 33.4

Portrait of the Artist's Sister,
Winifred 1898
Oil paint on canvas
45.7 × 40.6

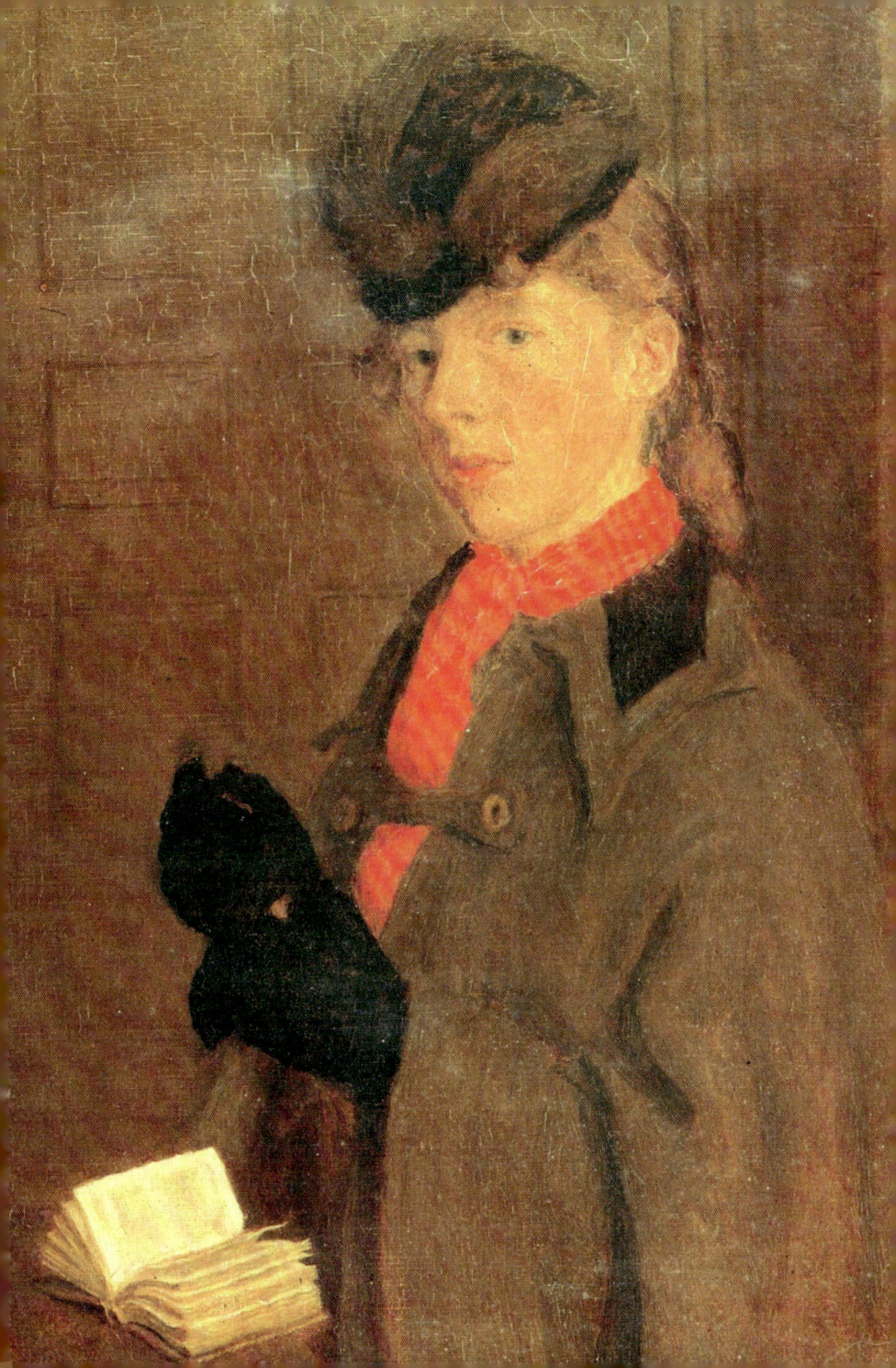

Portrait of Mrs Atkinson
c.1897–8
Oil paint on paperboard
30.5 × 31.1

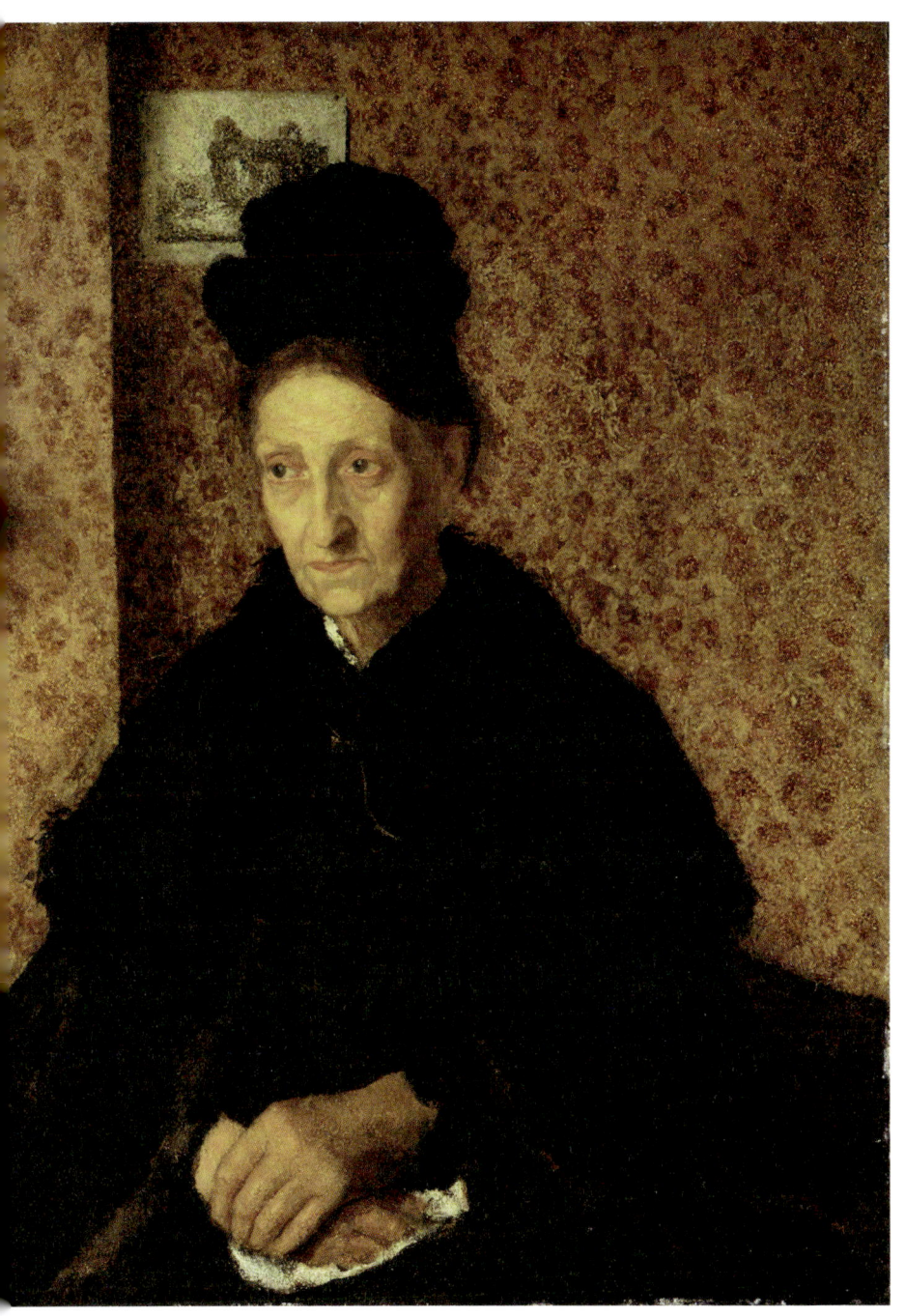

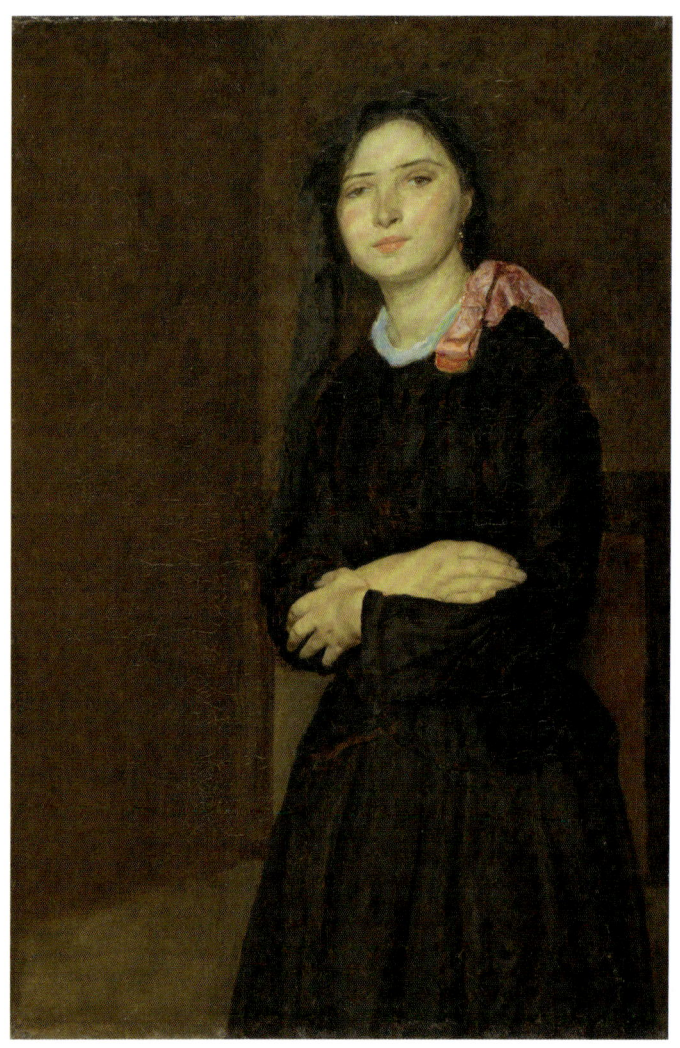

Dorelia in a Black Dress
c.1903–4
Oil paint on canvas
73 × 48.9

Autoportrait à la Lettre
c.1907–9
Watercolour and graphite
on paper
22.3 × 16.1

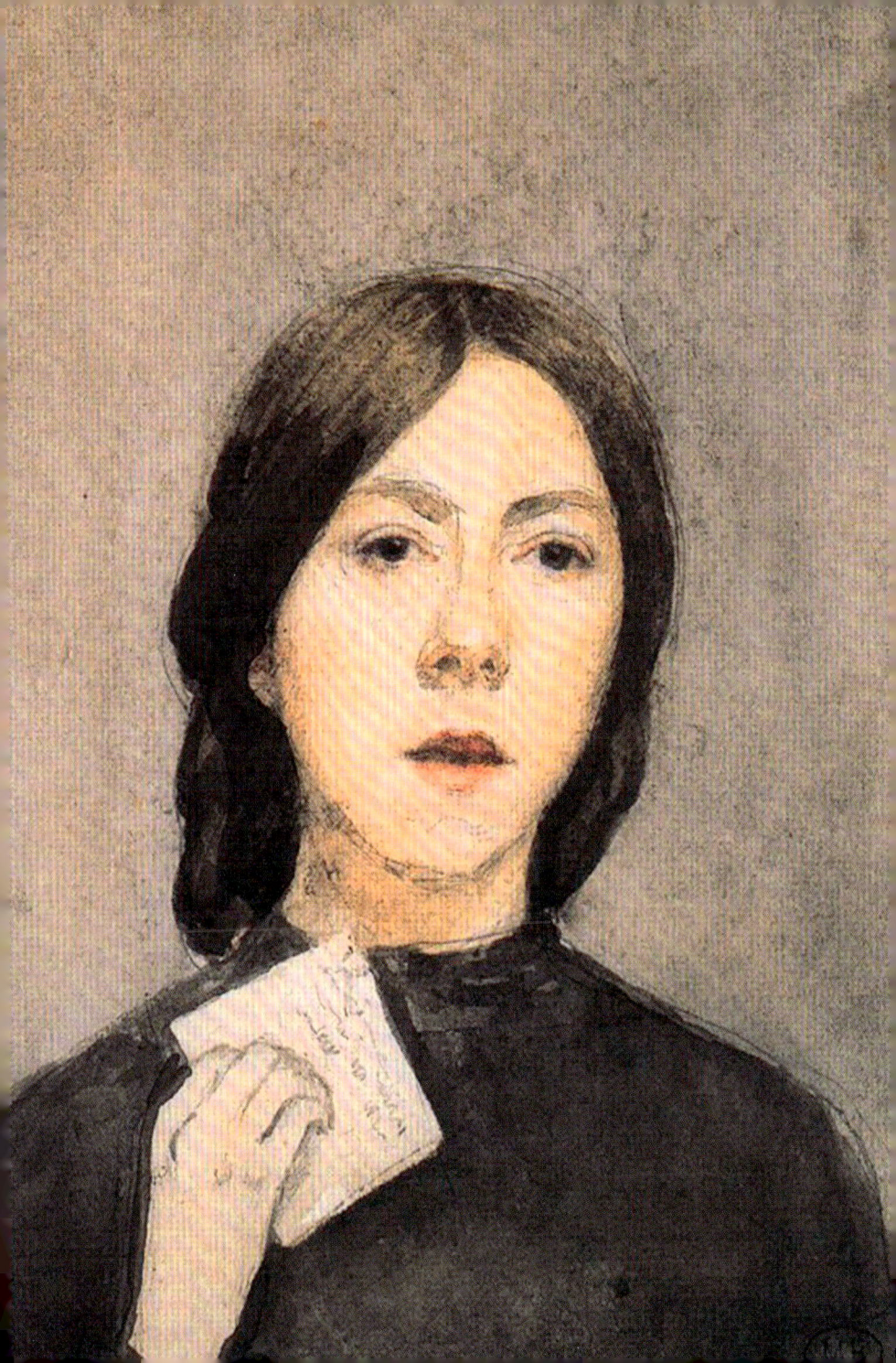

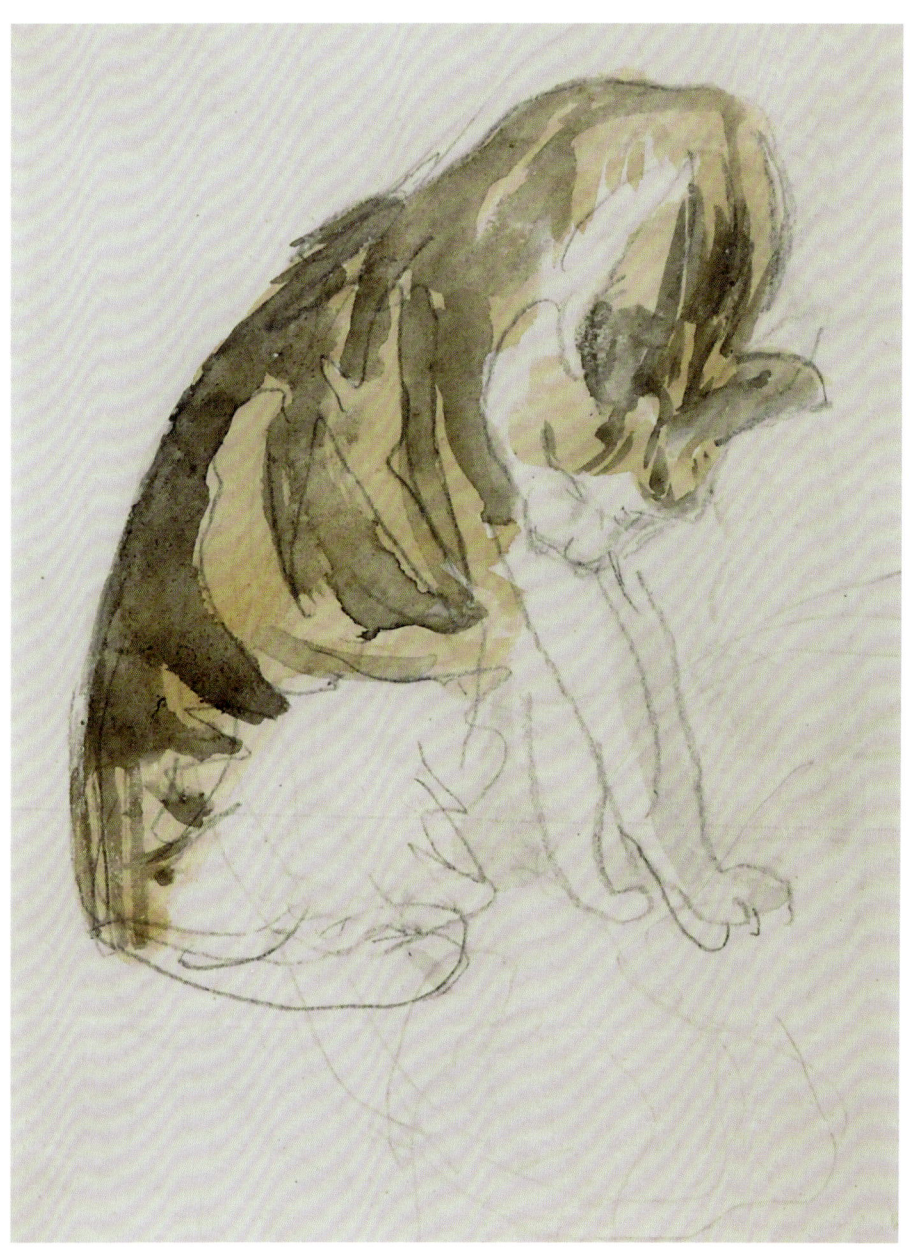

Cat c.1904–8
Graphite and watercolour
on paper
16.5 × 11.7

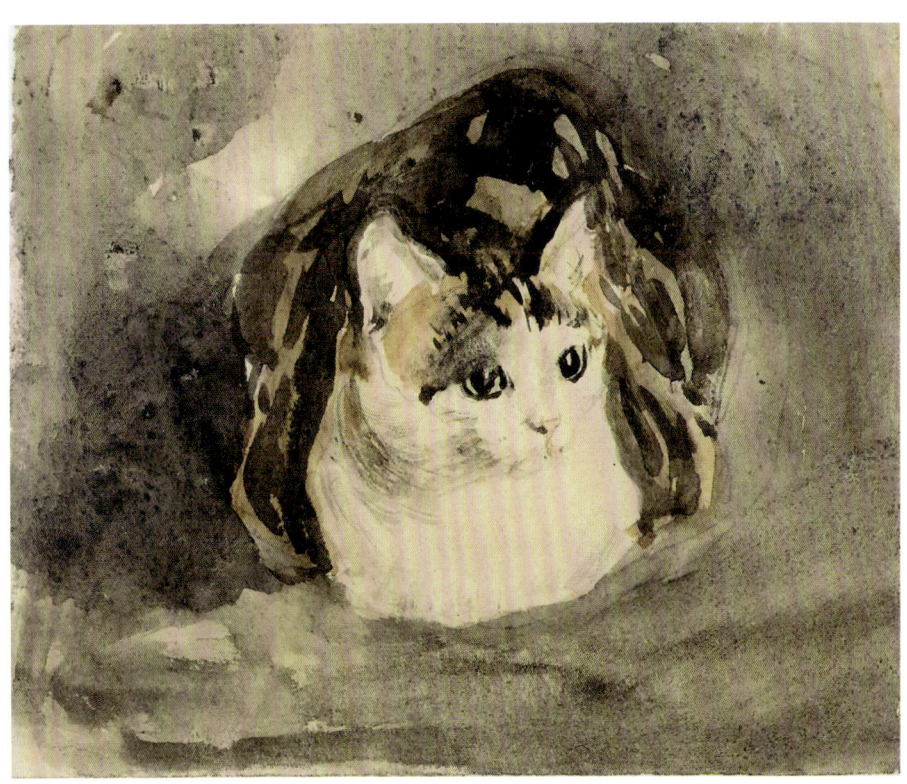

Cat c.1904–8
Graphite and watercolour
on paper
11.1 × 13.7

OVERLEAF
Cat c.1904–8
Graphite and watercolour
on paper
12.3 × 16

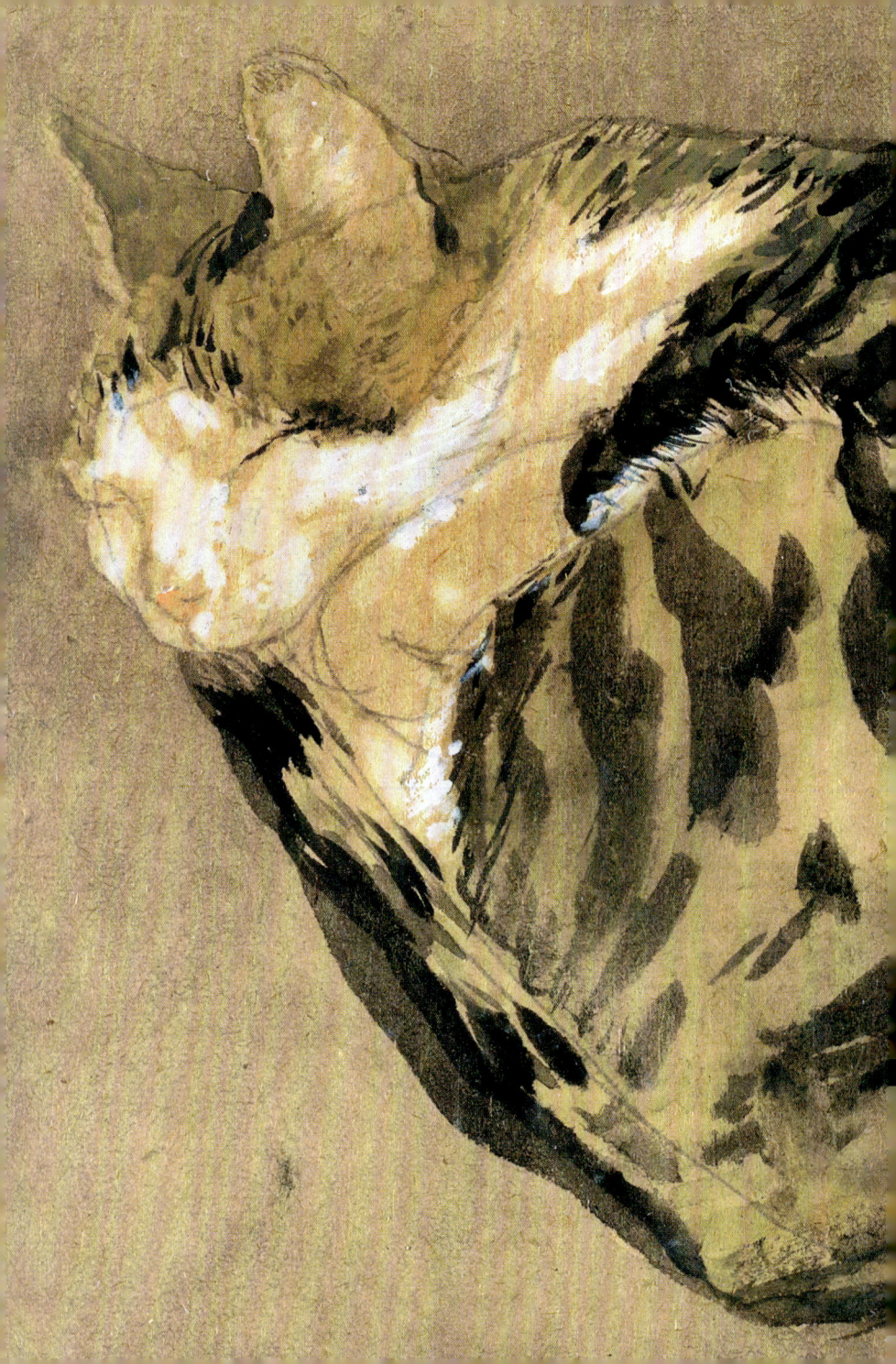

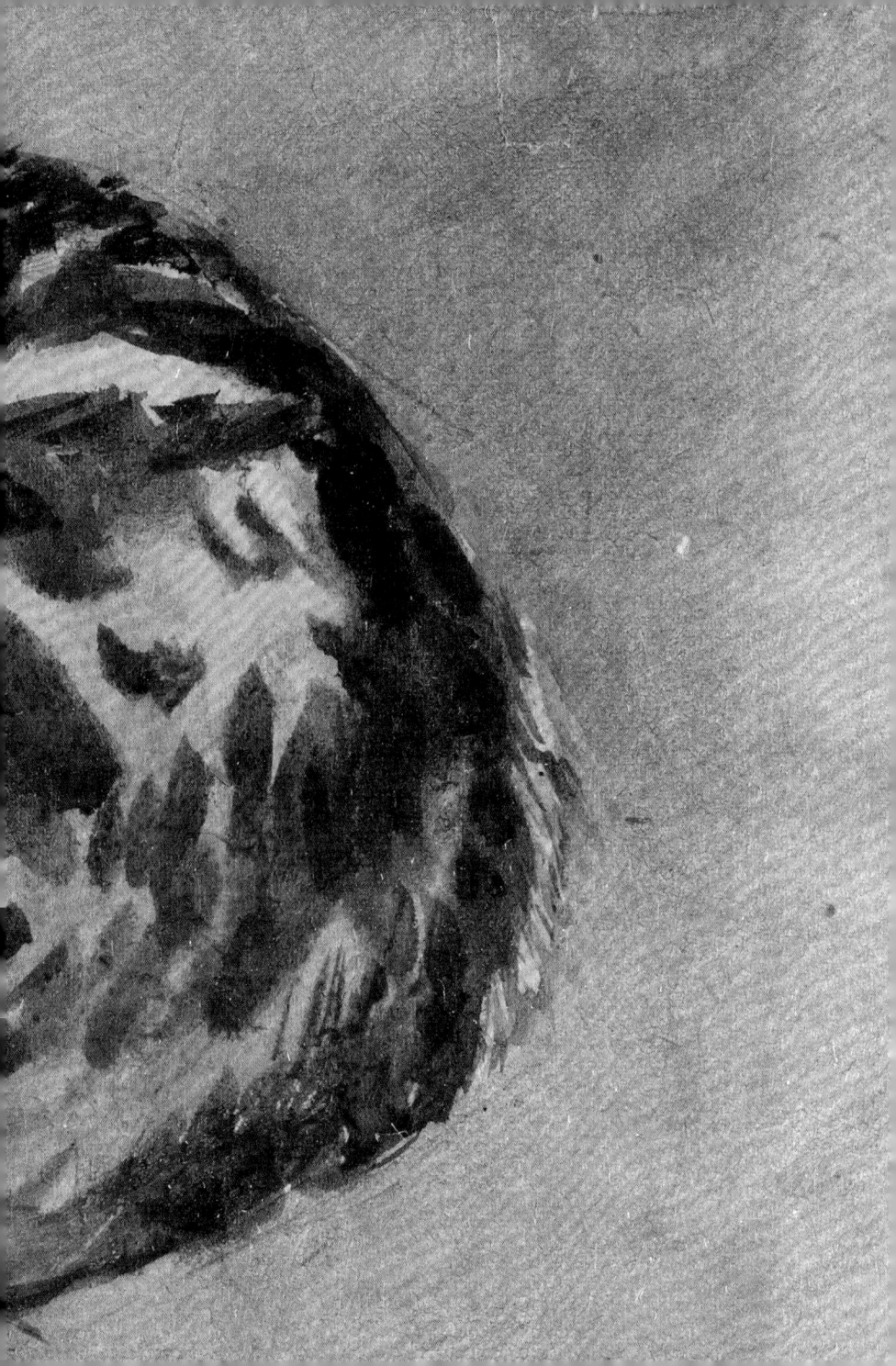

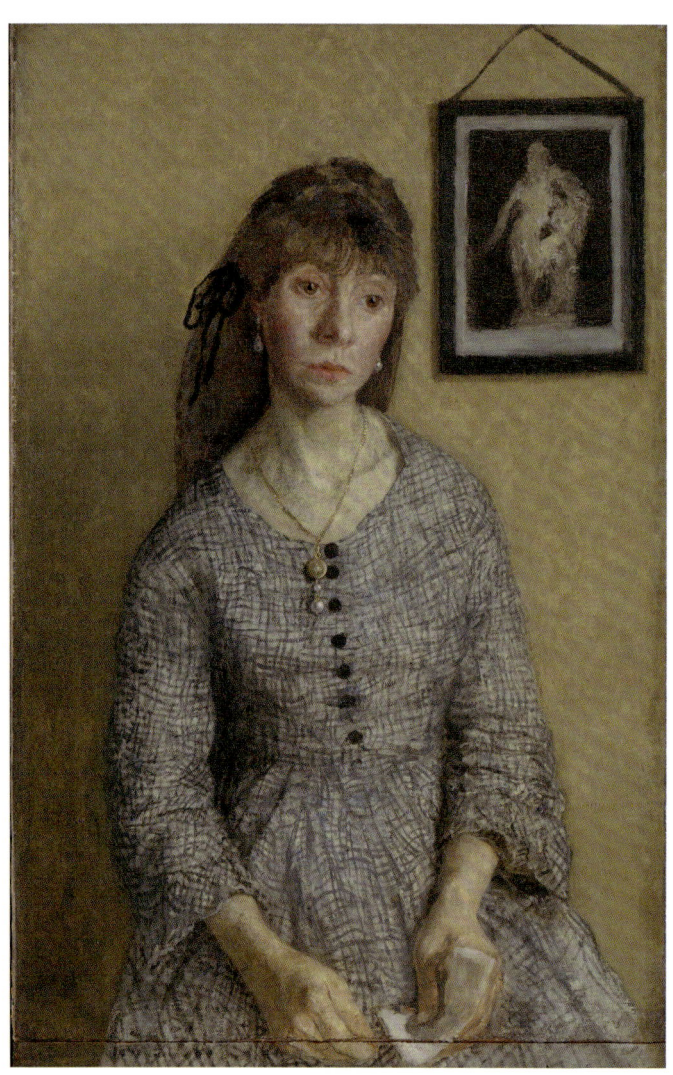

Chloë Boughton-Leigh c.1907
Oil paint on canvas
58.4 × 38.1

Chloë Boughton-Leigh 1910
Oil paint on canvas
60.3 × 38.1

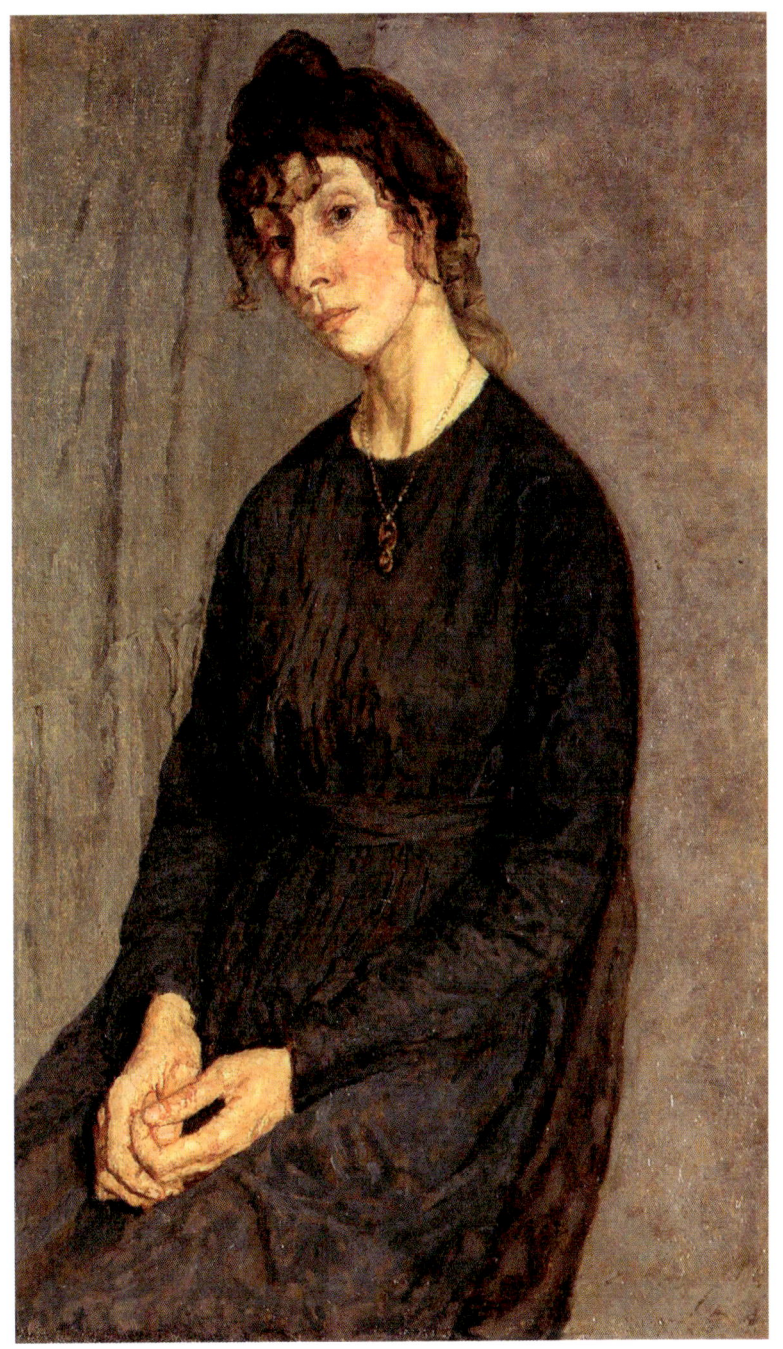

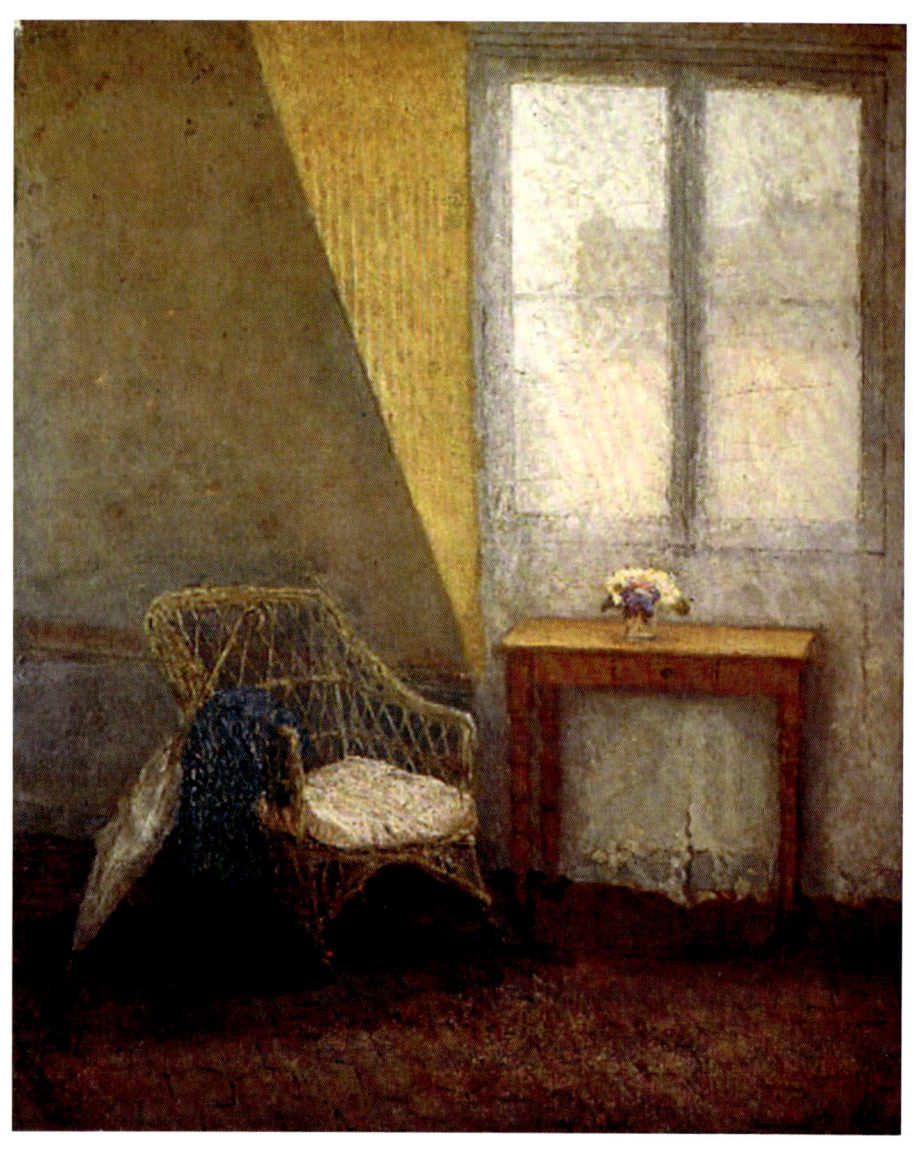

*A Corner of the Artist's Room in
Paris* 1907–9
Oil paint on canvas
31.7 × 26.7

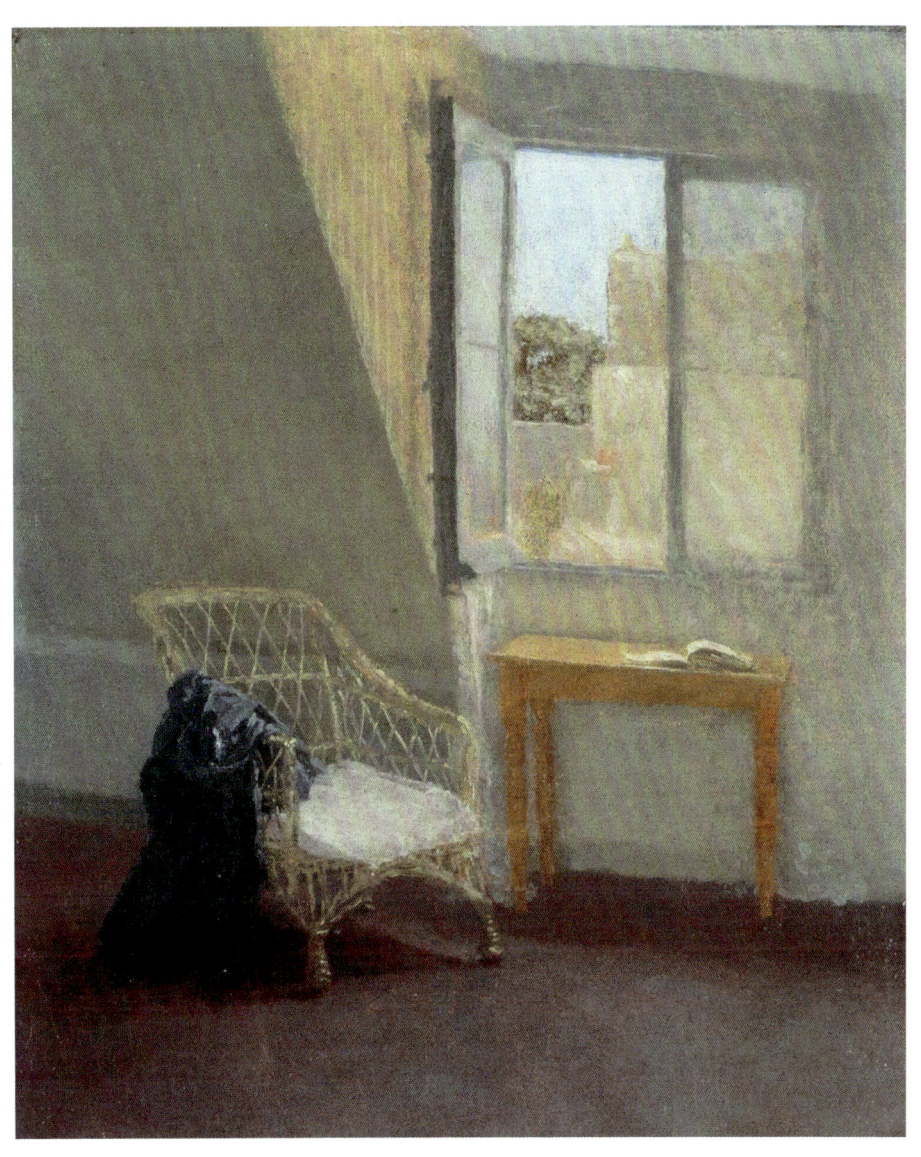

A Corner of the Artist's Room
in Paris (with Open Window)
1907–9
Oil paint on canvas
31.2 × 24.8

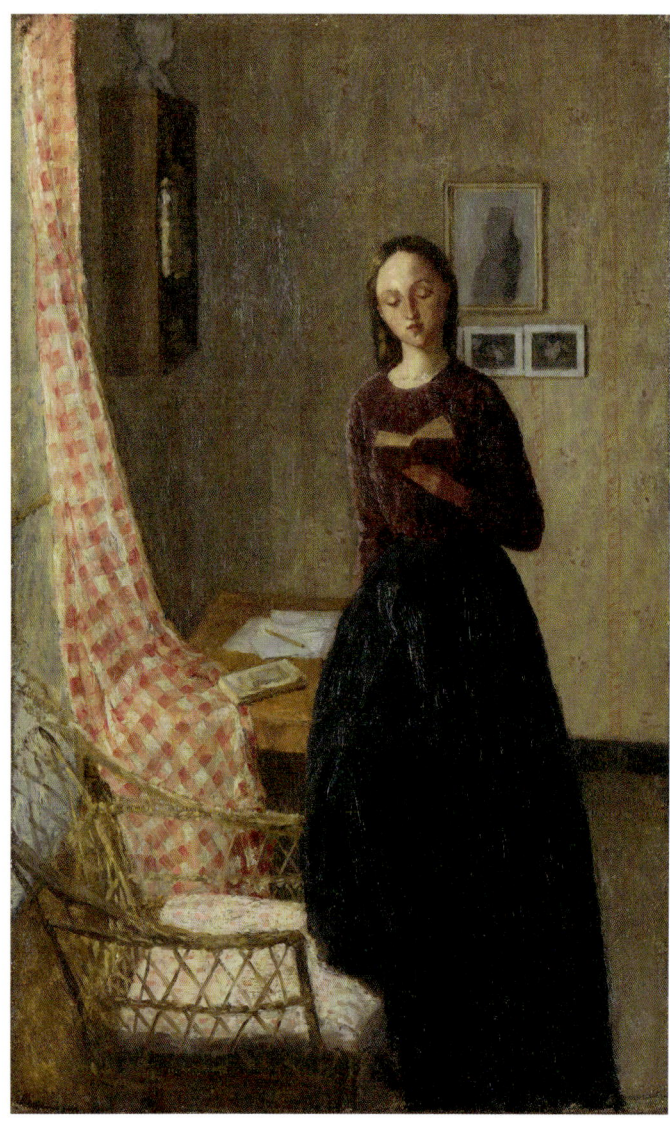

A Lady Reading c.1910–11
Oil paint on canvas
40.3 × 25.4

Girl Reading at the Window
1911
Oil paint on canvas
40.9 × 25.3

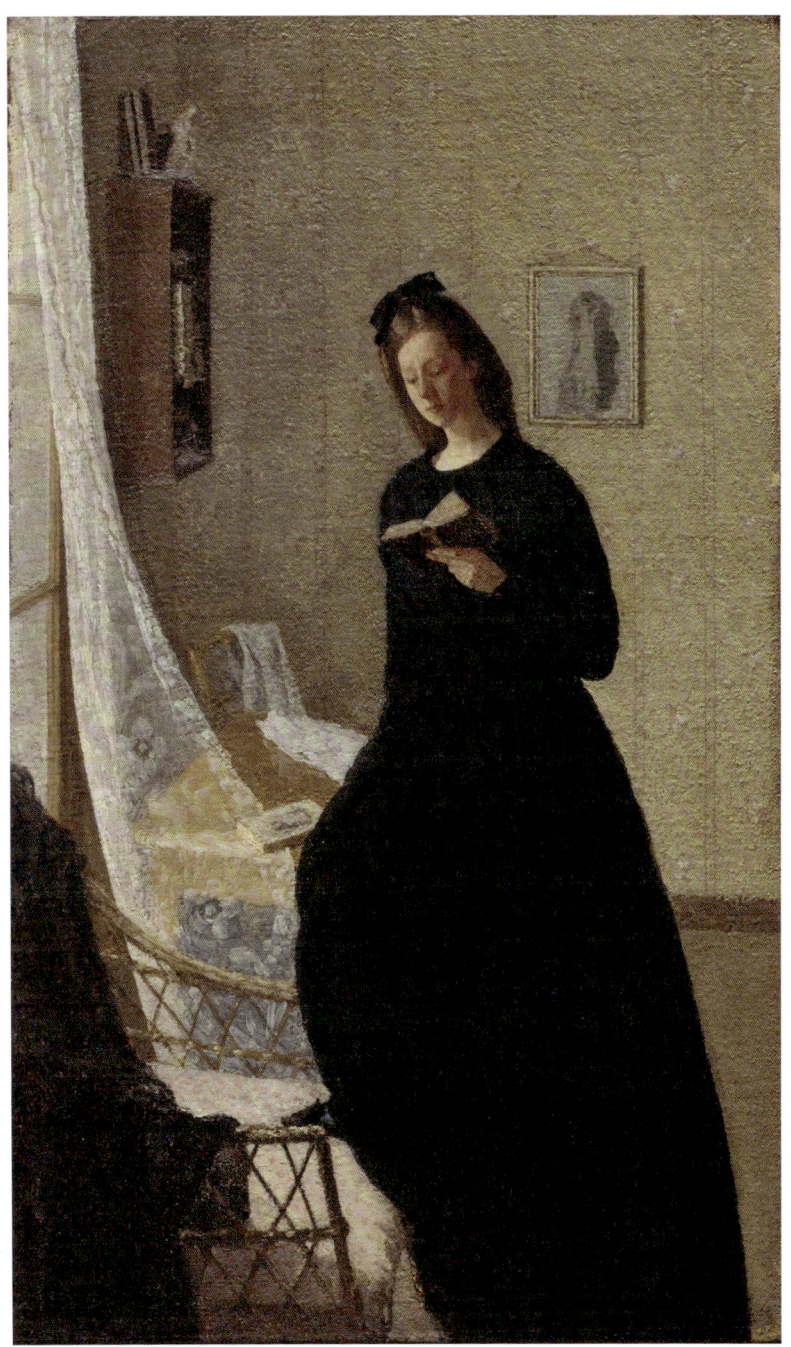

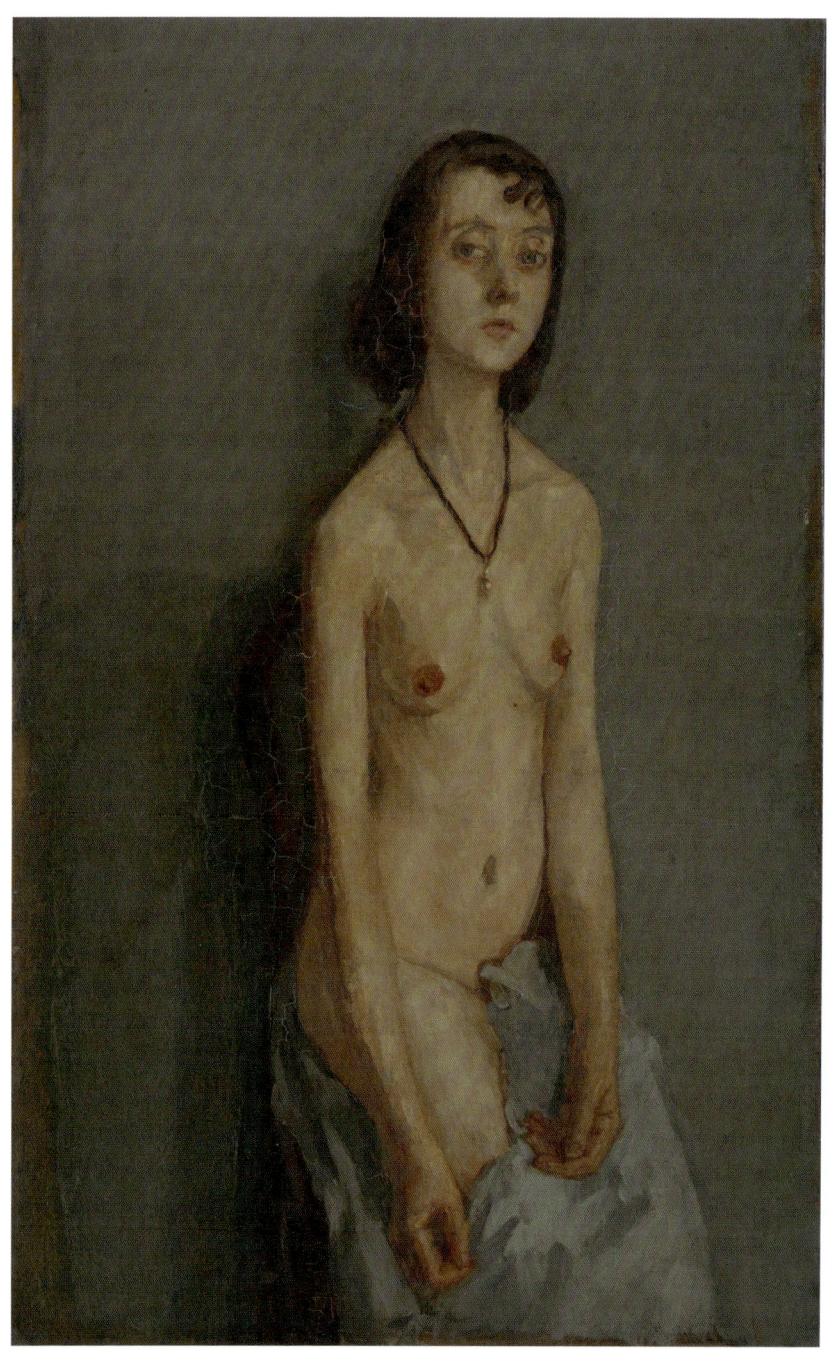

Nude Girl 1909–10
Oil paint on canvas
44.5 × 27.9

Girl with Bare Shoulders
1909–10
Oil paint on canvas
43.4 × 26

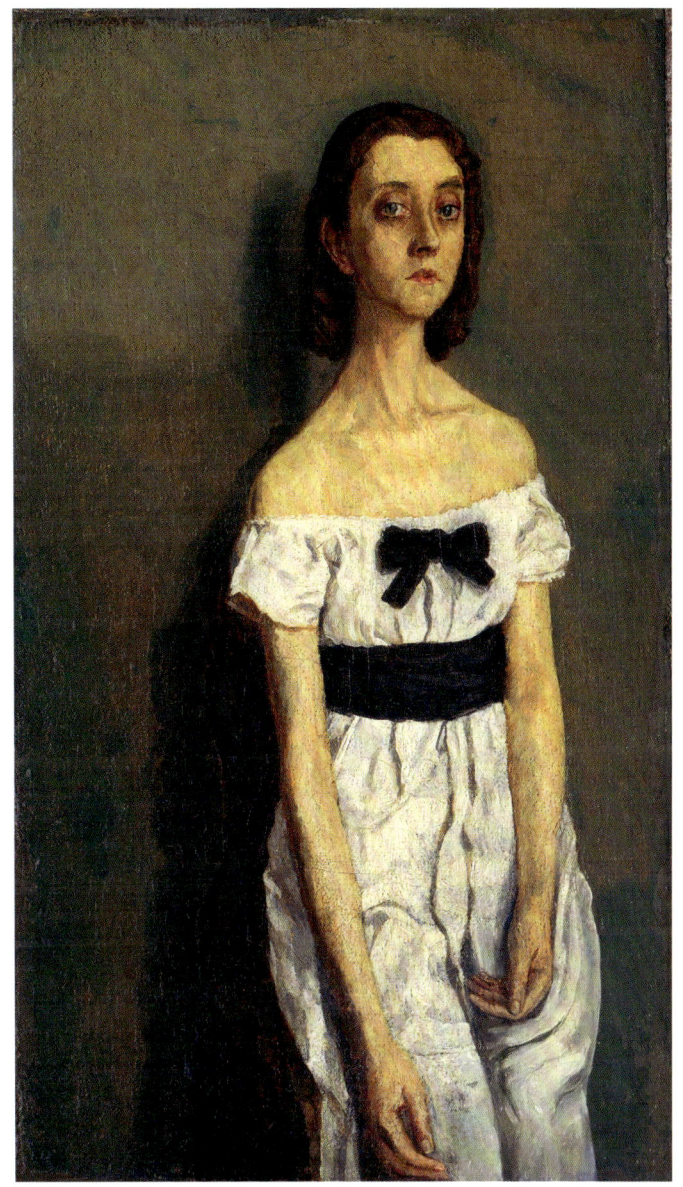

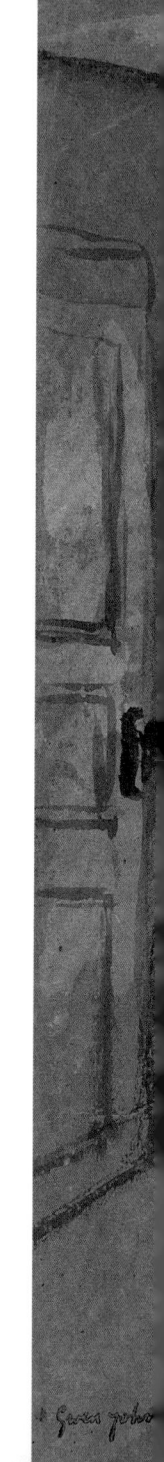

Woman Dressing c.1907
Grey wash and white
gouache on slightly
textured brown paper
27.6 × 23.2

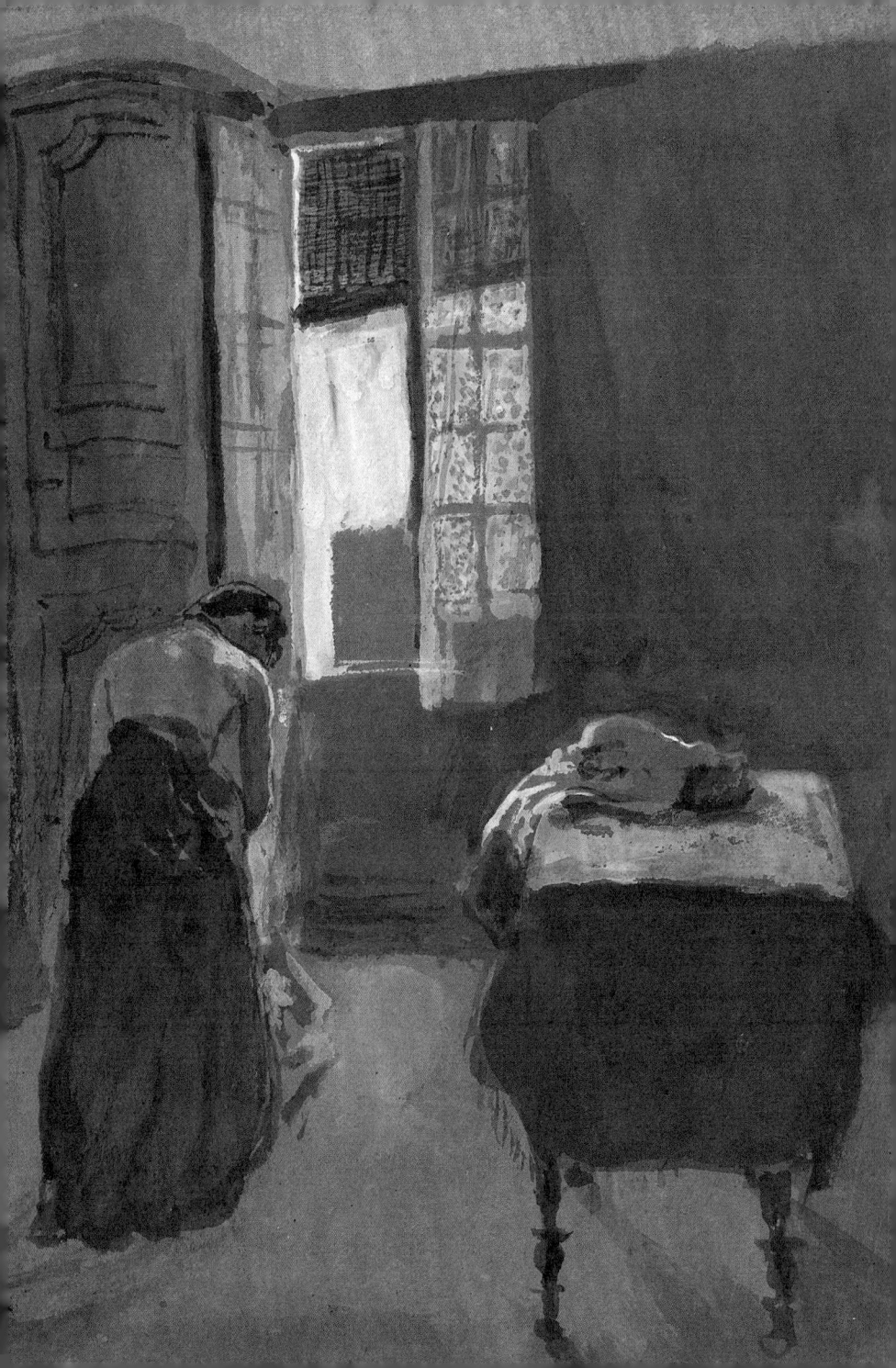

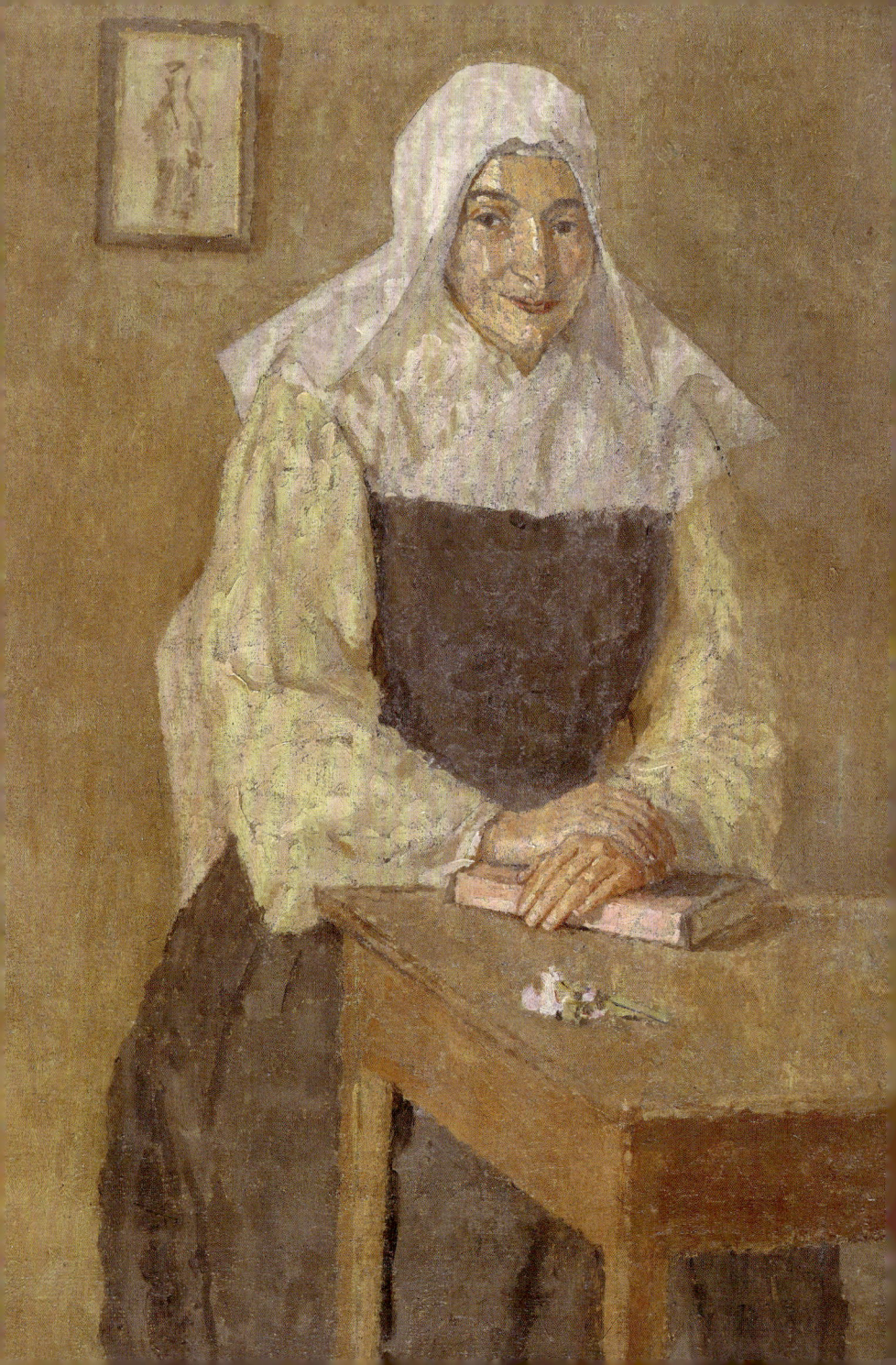

Mère Poussepin Seated at a Table c.1915
Oil paint on canvas
88.3 × 65.4

The Nun late 1910s
Oil paint on board
70.7 × 46.6

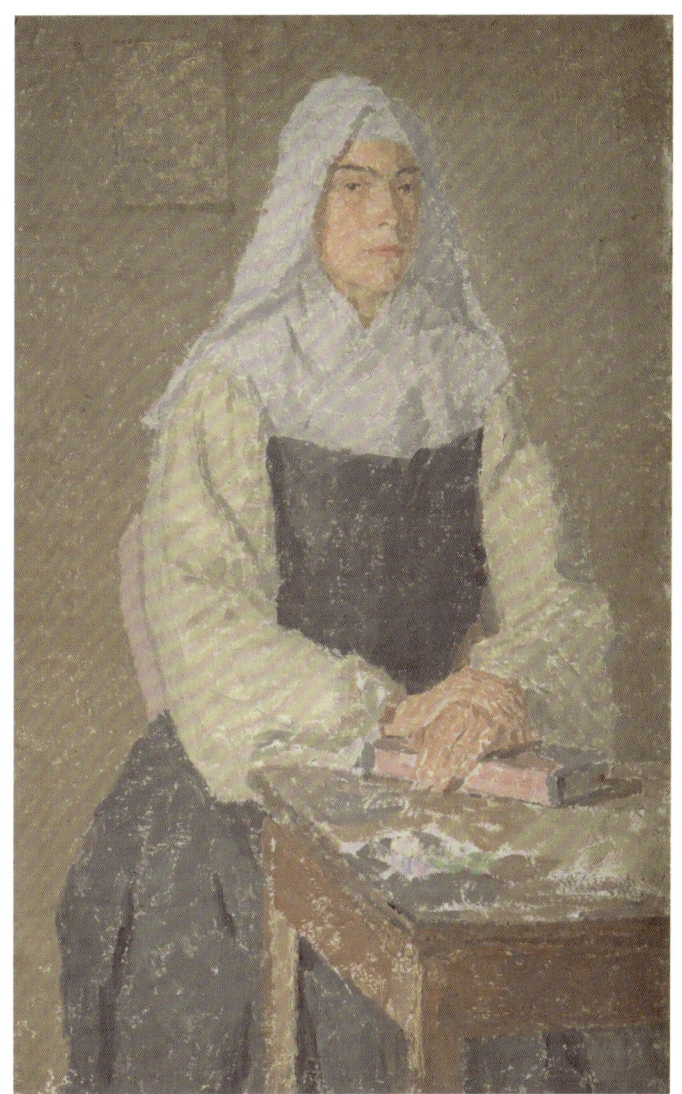

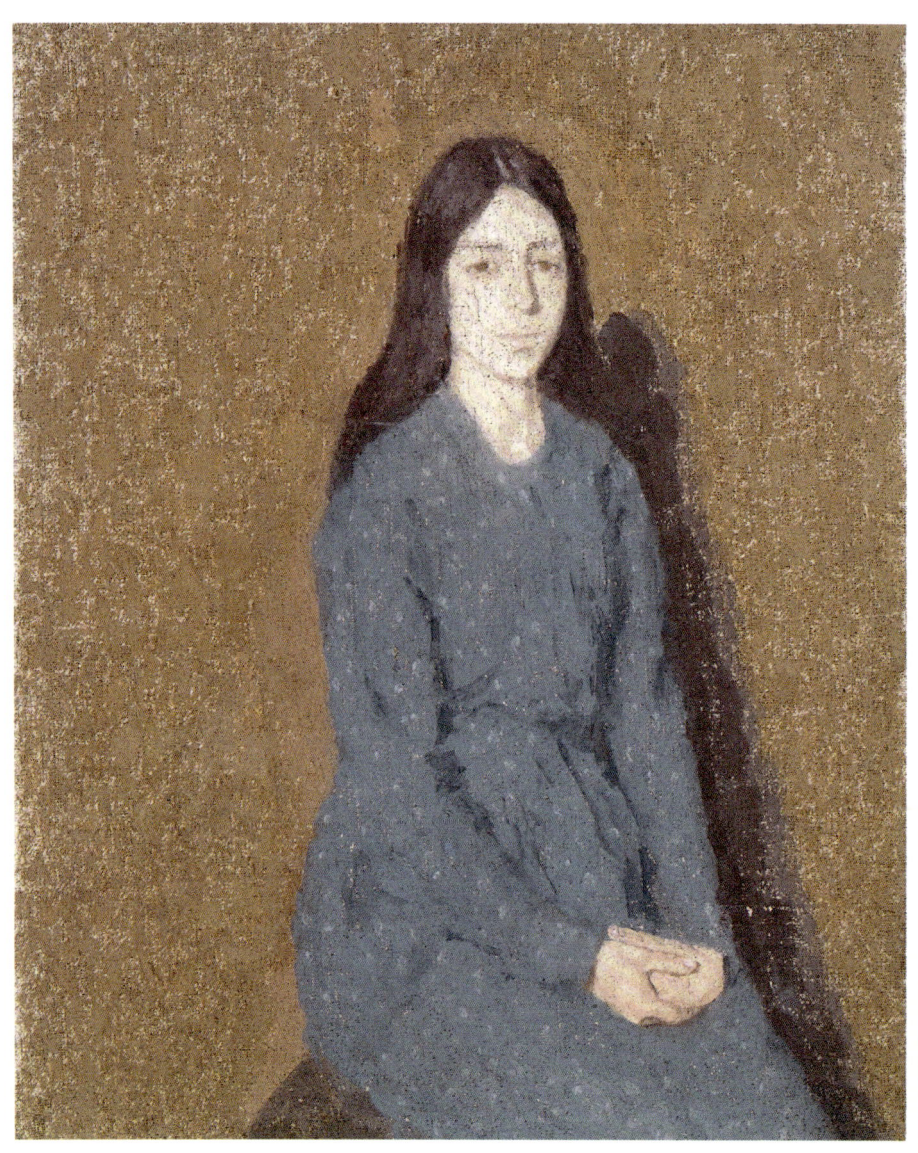

Girl in a Blue Dress c.1914–5
Oil paint on canvas
35.1 × 27

Study of a Child c.1915–20
Watercolour on paper
32.4 × 25.1

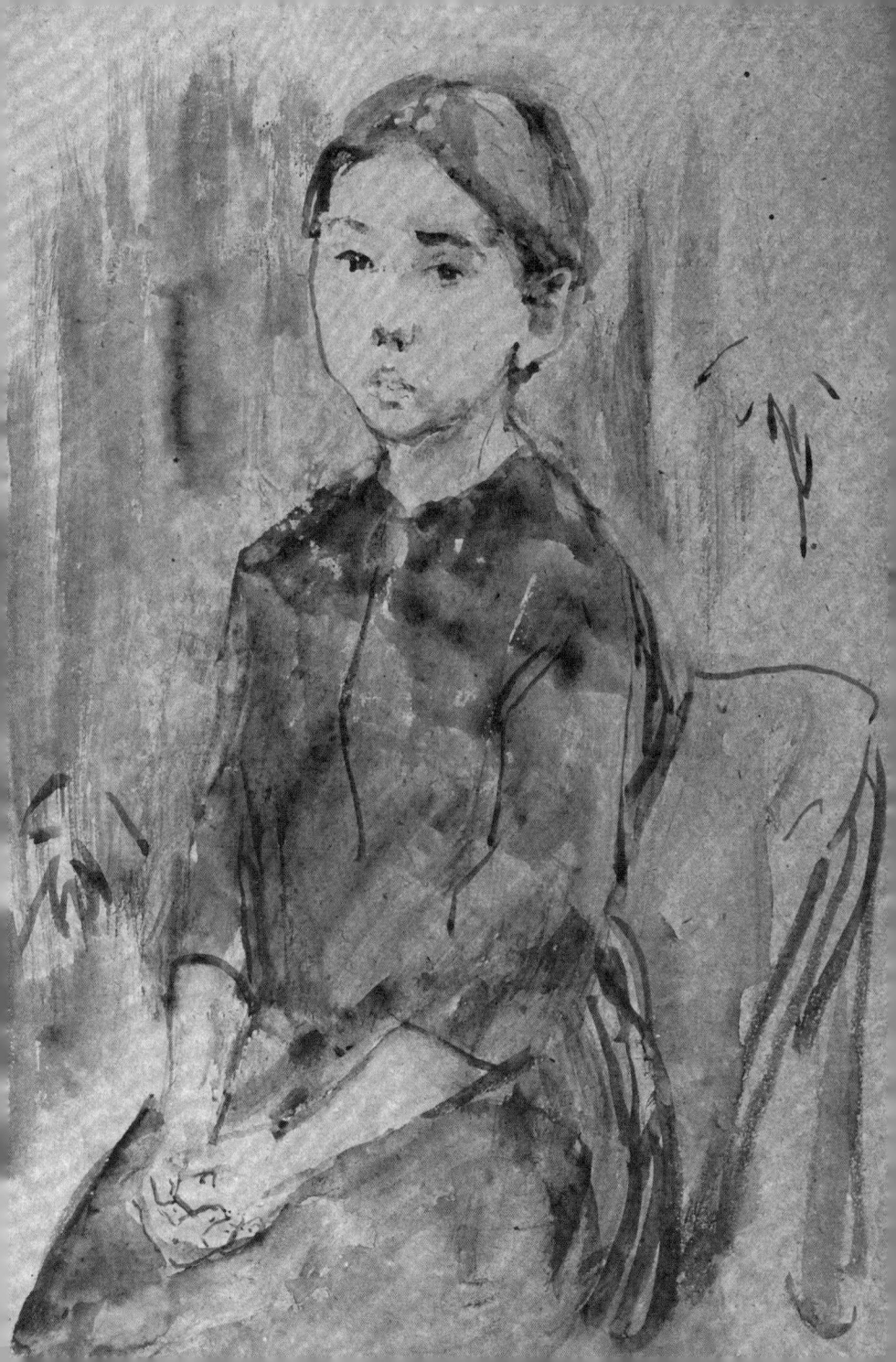

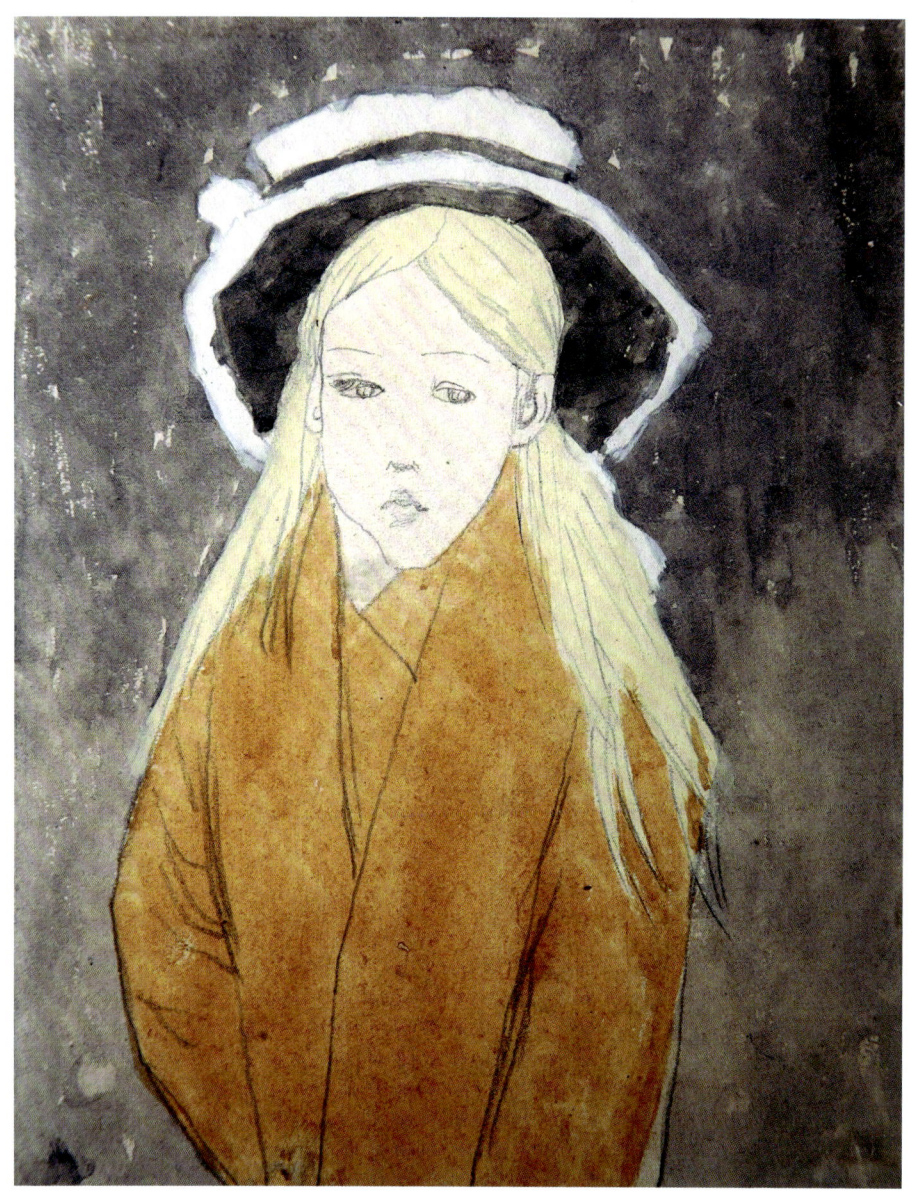

Little Girl Wearing a Straw Hat
late 1910s
Watercolour on paper
21.6 × 17.2

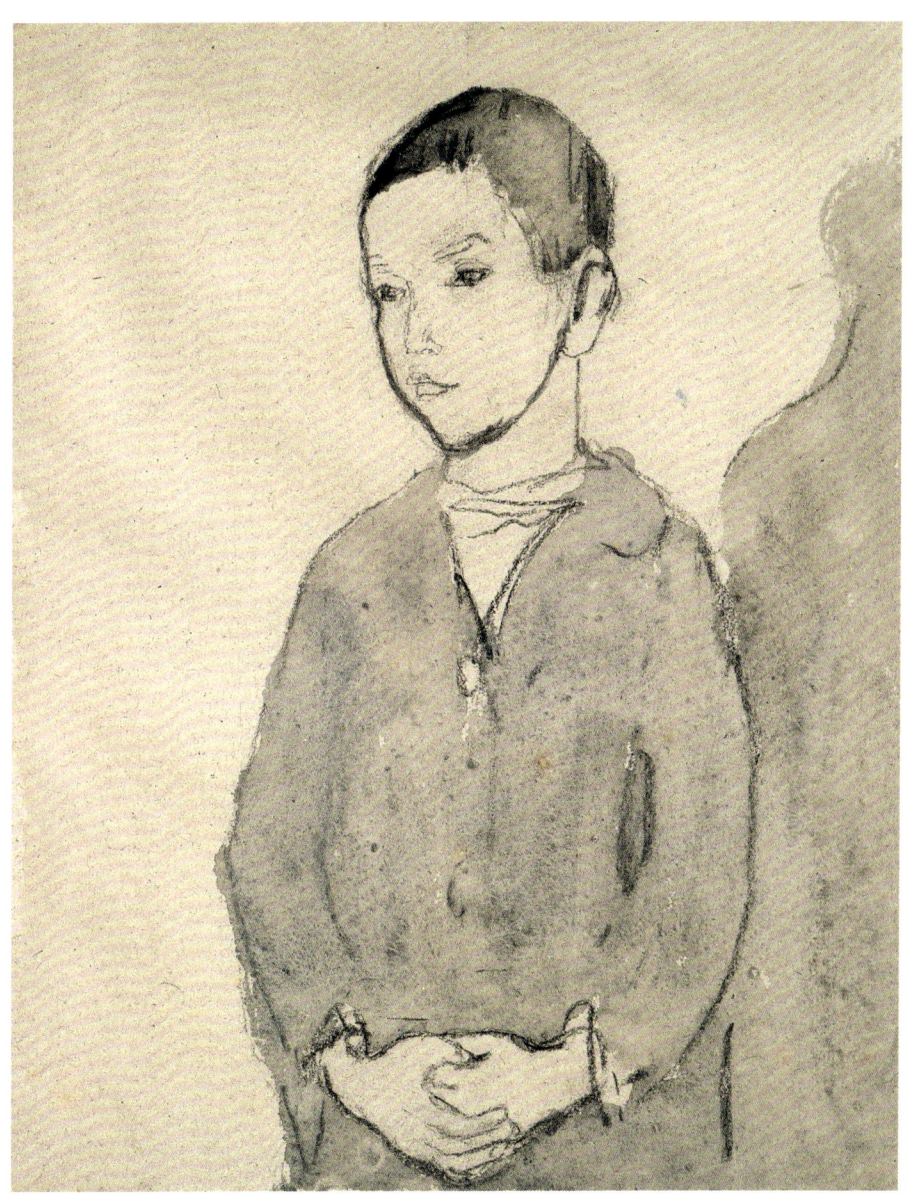

Boy with Clasped Hands
c.late 1910s
Charcoal on grey paper
32.5 × 23.7

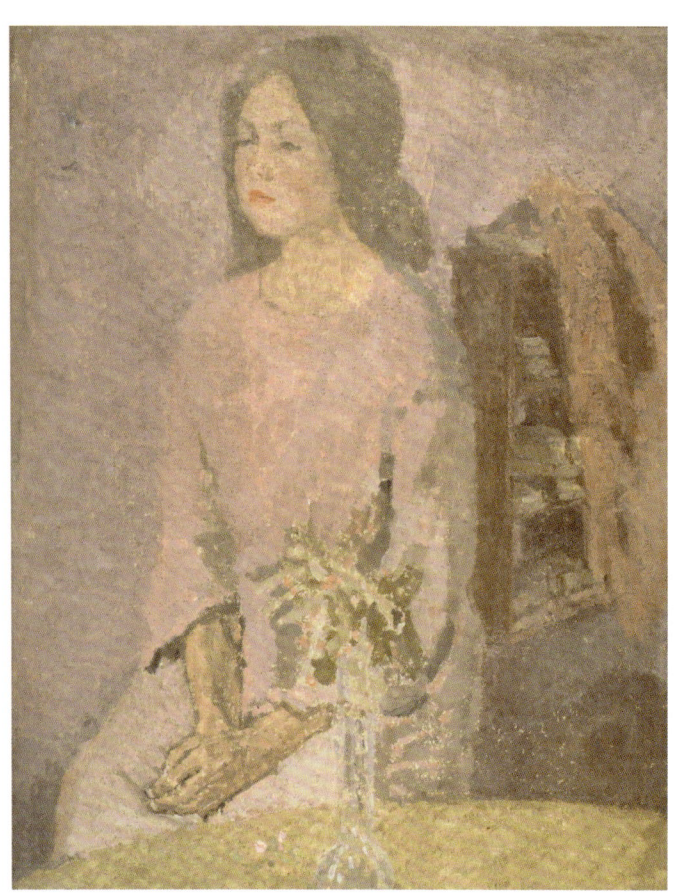

Girl in Rose early 1920s
Oil paint on canvas
46.3 × 36.2

Girl in Profile late 1910s
Oil paint on canvas
45.7 × 31.7

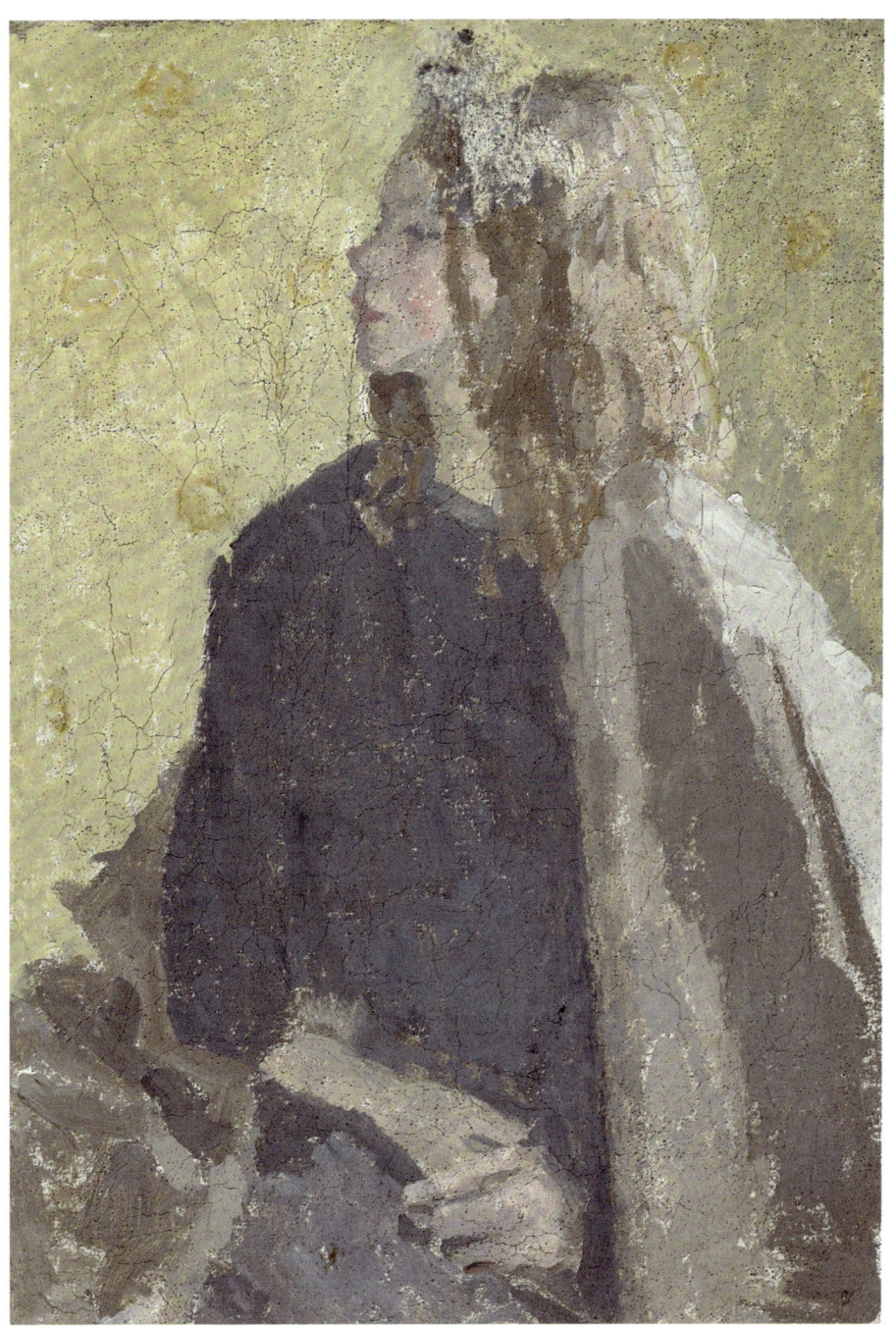

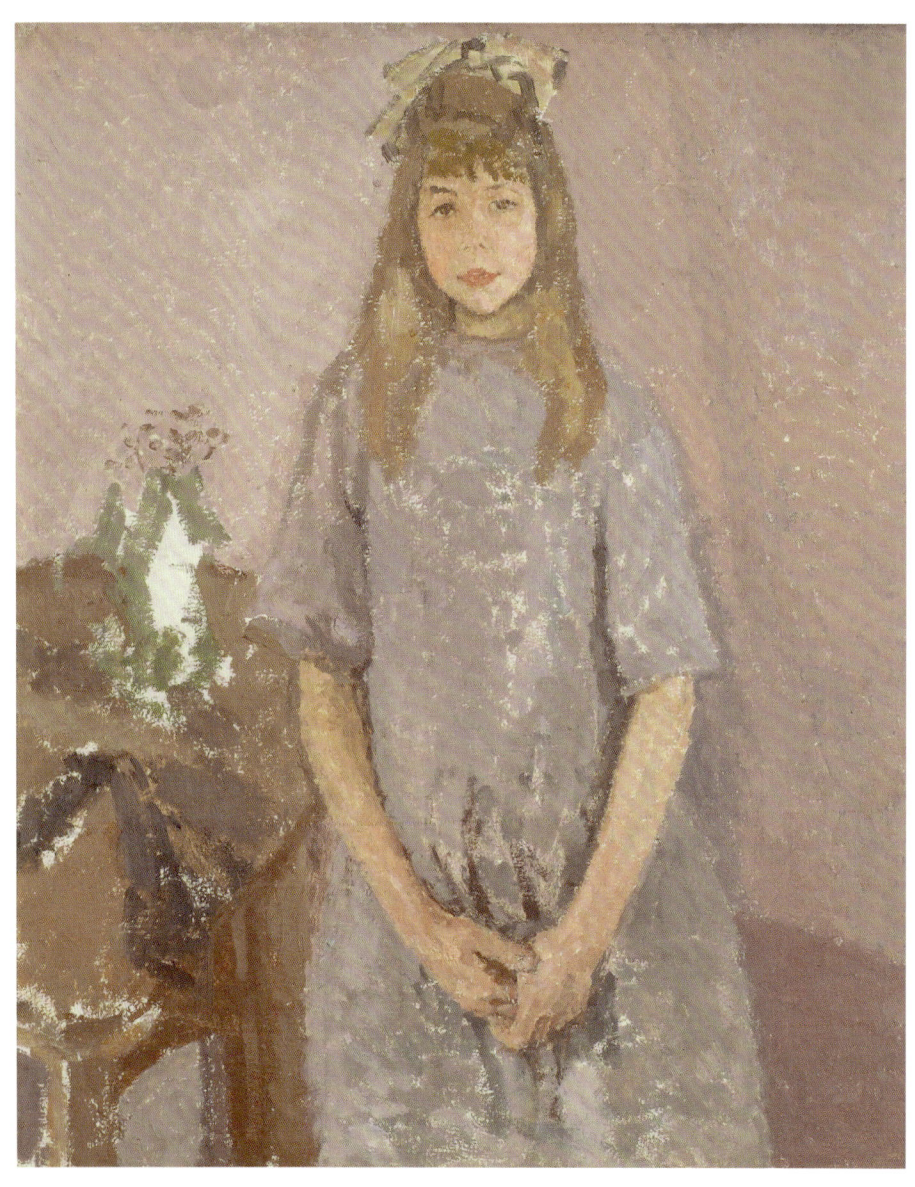

La Petite Modèle late 1910s
Oil paint on canvas
56.4 × 45.7

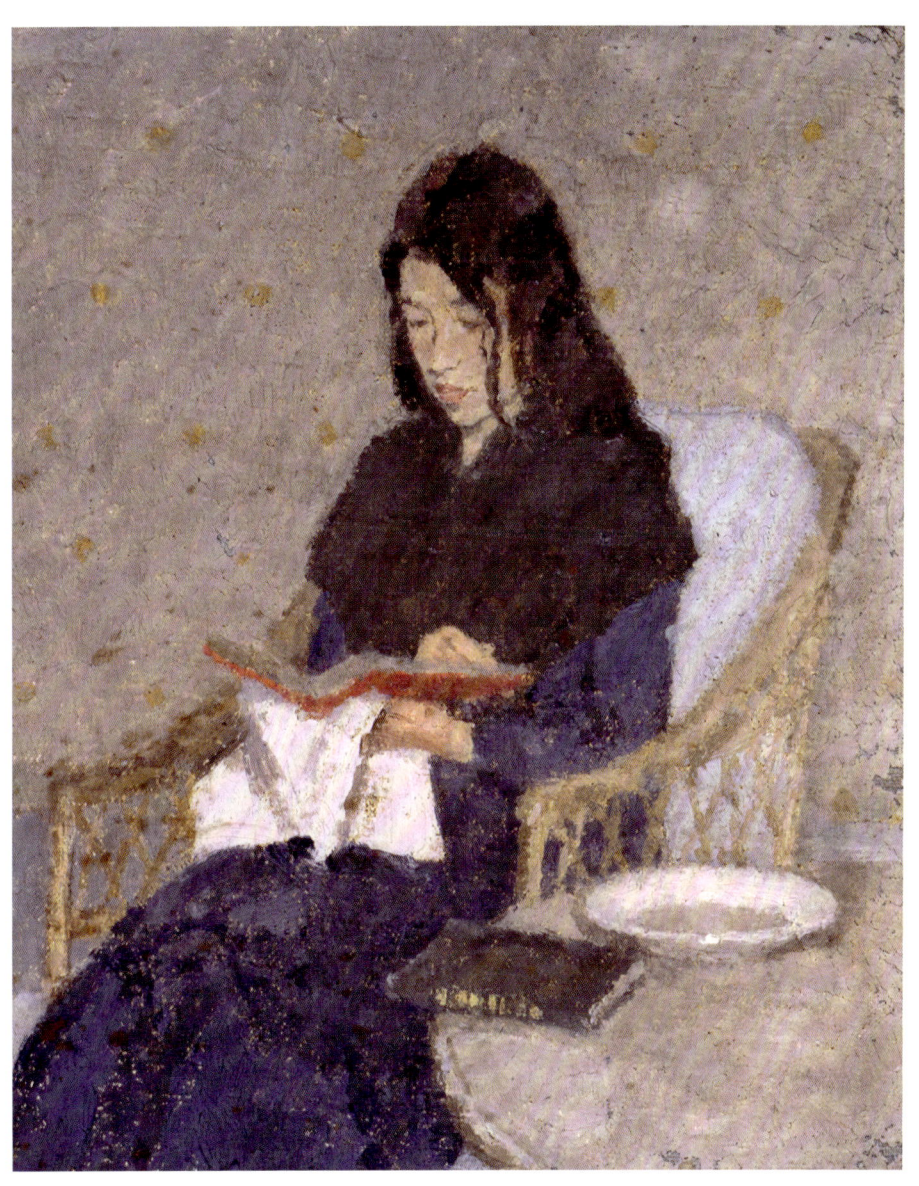

The Seated Woman
late 1910s–mid 1920s
Oil paint on canvas
27.7 × 22.5

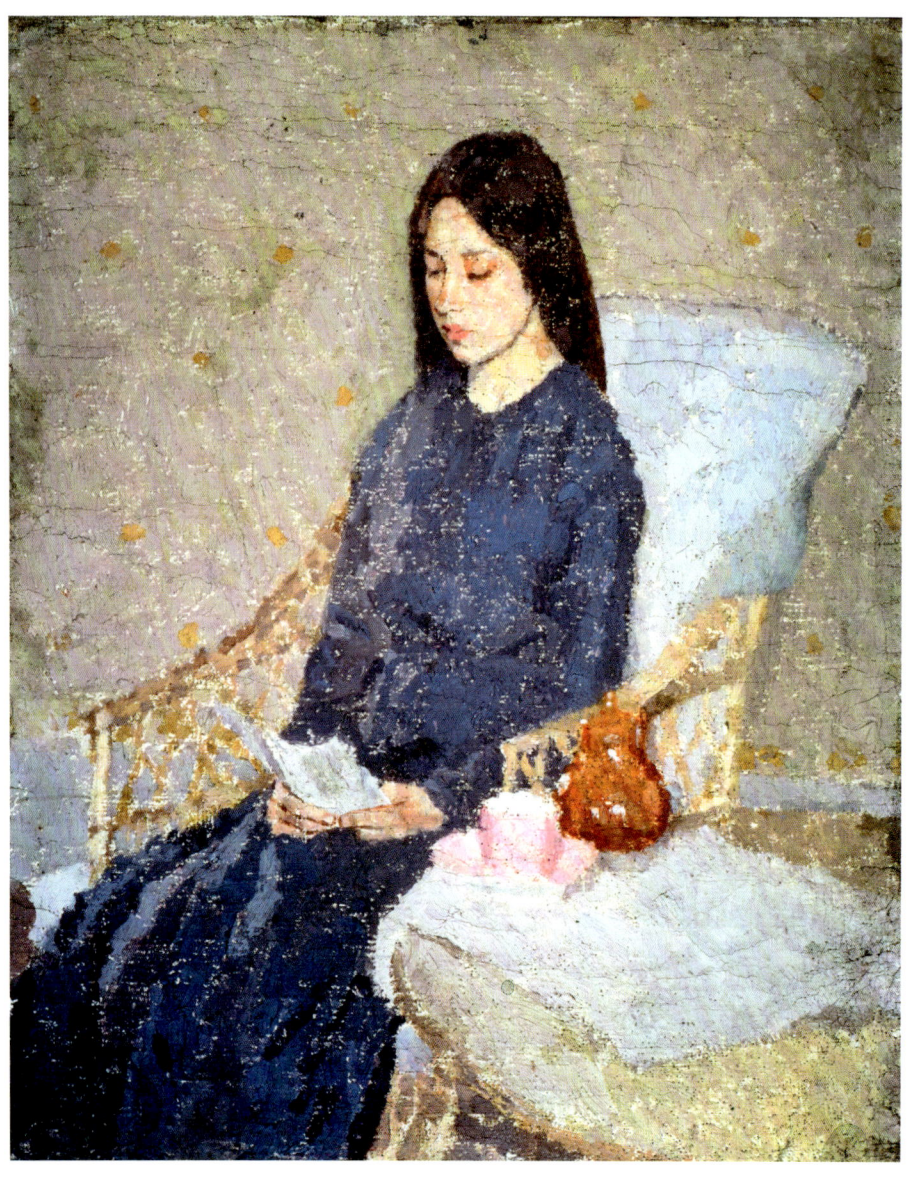

The Convalescent
late 1910s–mid 1920s
Oil paint on canvas
41.2 × 33

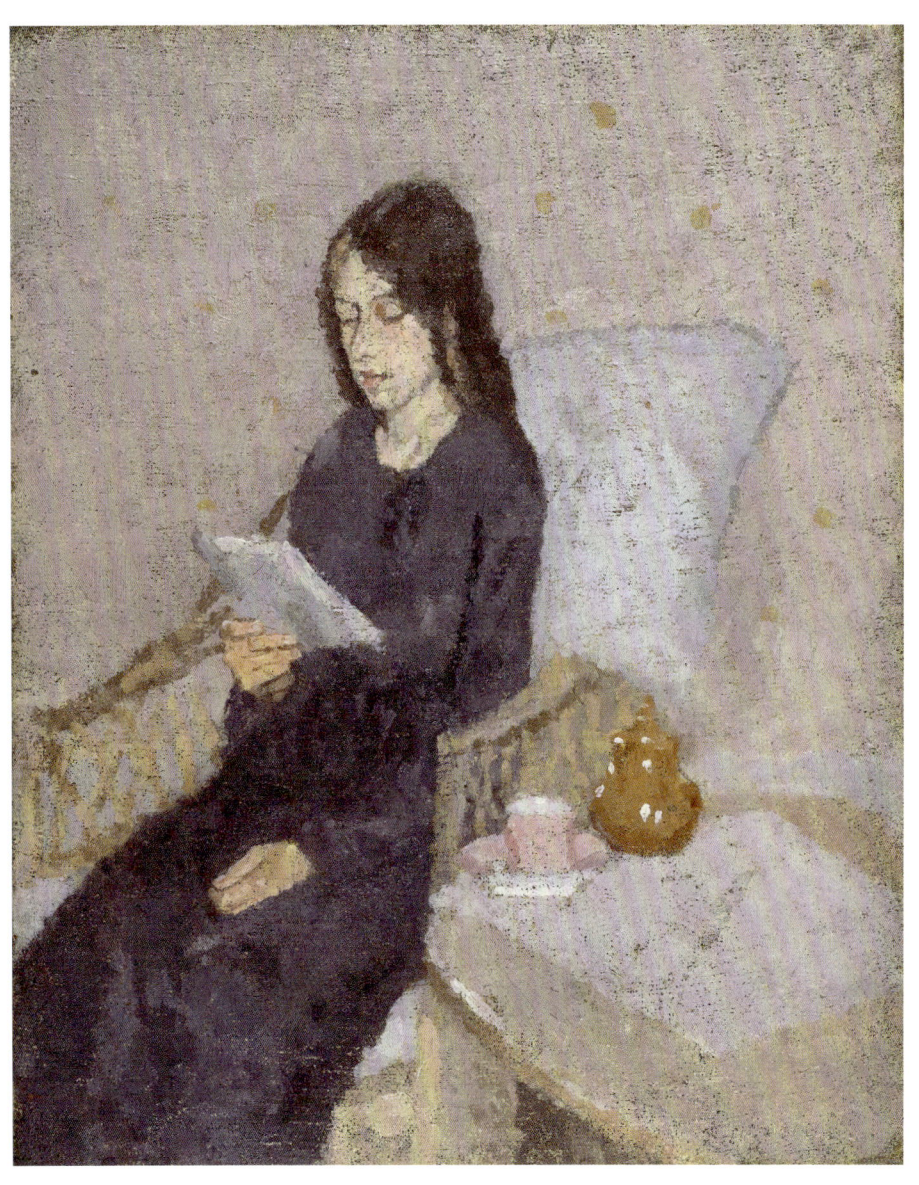

The Letter c.1924
Oil paint on canvas
41.9 × 33.2

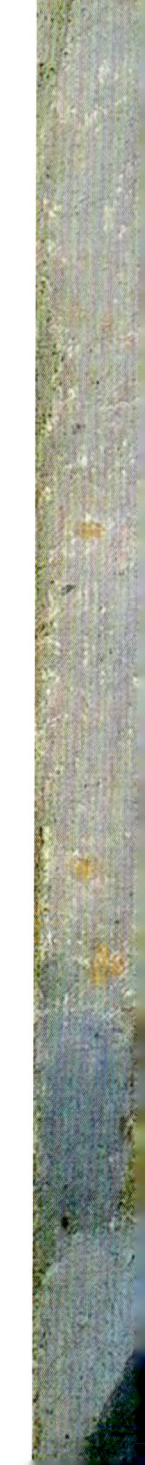

The Precious Book
1910s–mid 1920s
Oil paint on canvas
26.7 × 22.2

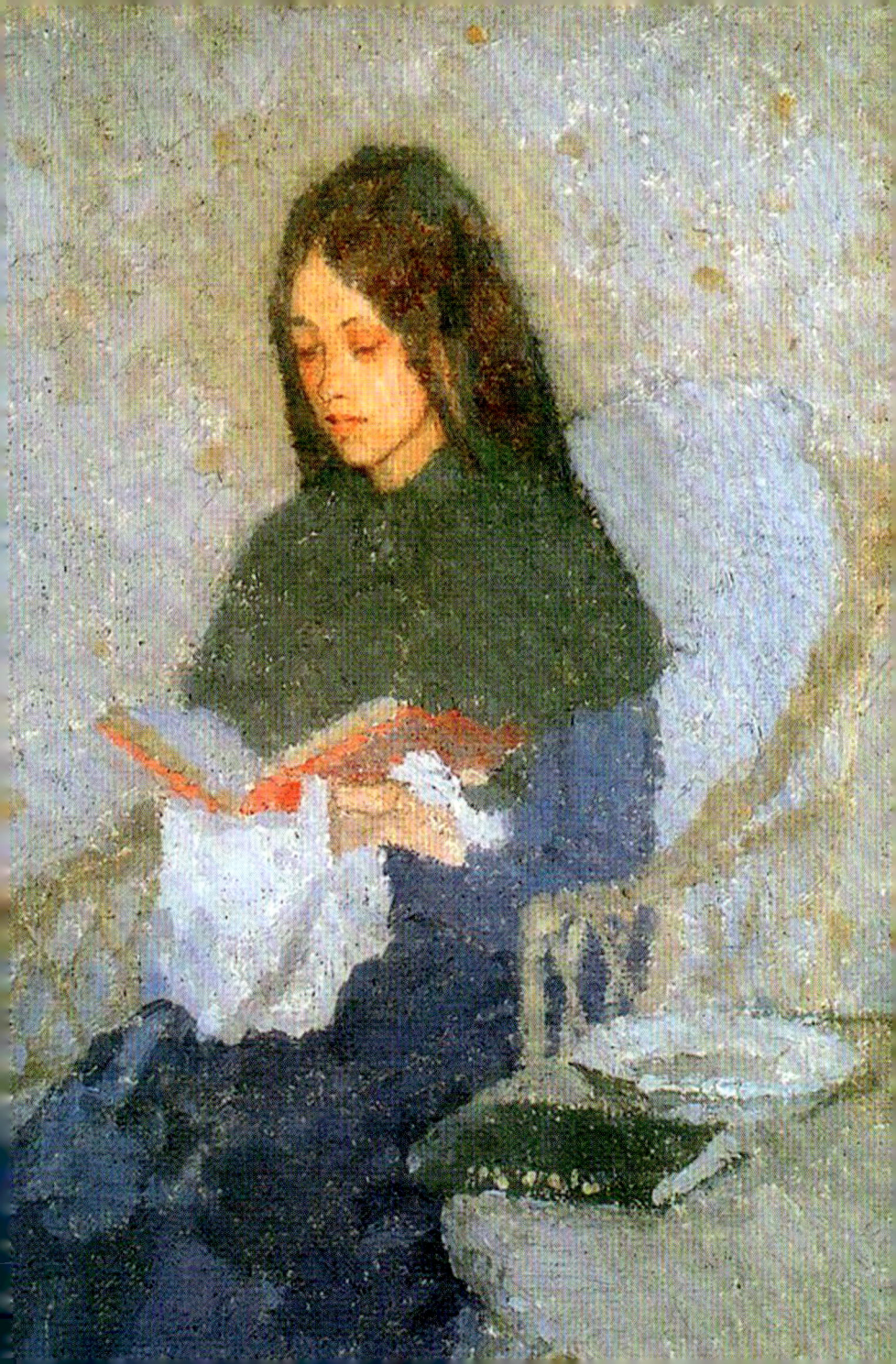

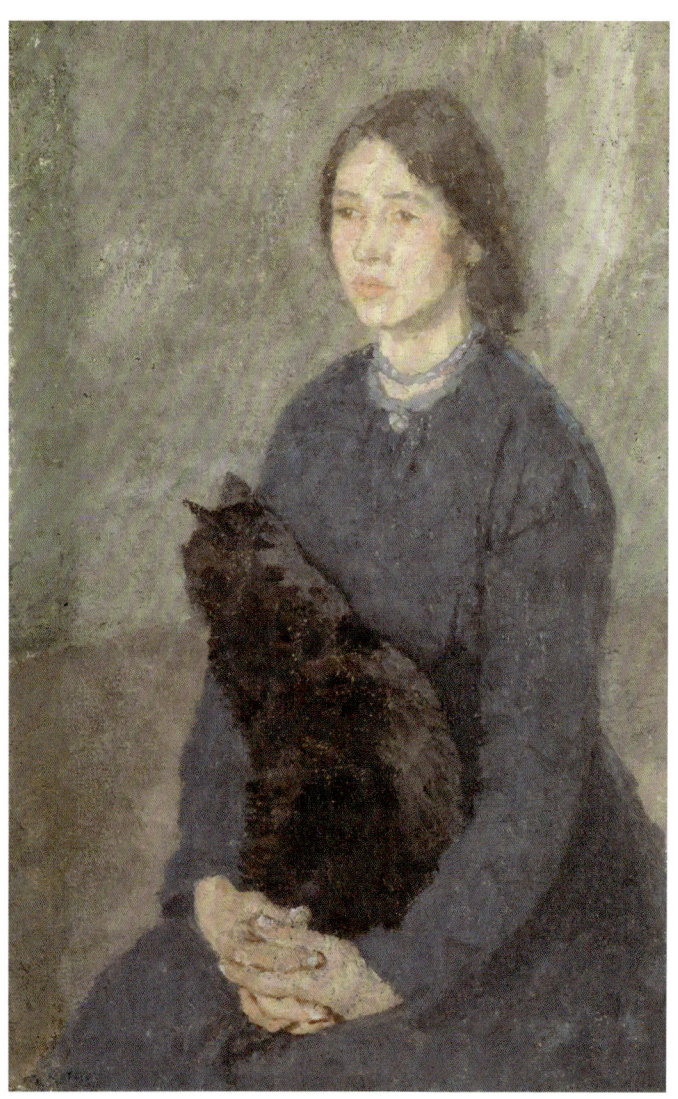

*Young Woman Holding a Black
Cat* late 1910s–early 1920s
Oil paint on canvas
46 × 29.8

Girl with a Cat 1918–22
Oil paint on canvas
33.7 × 26.7

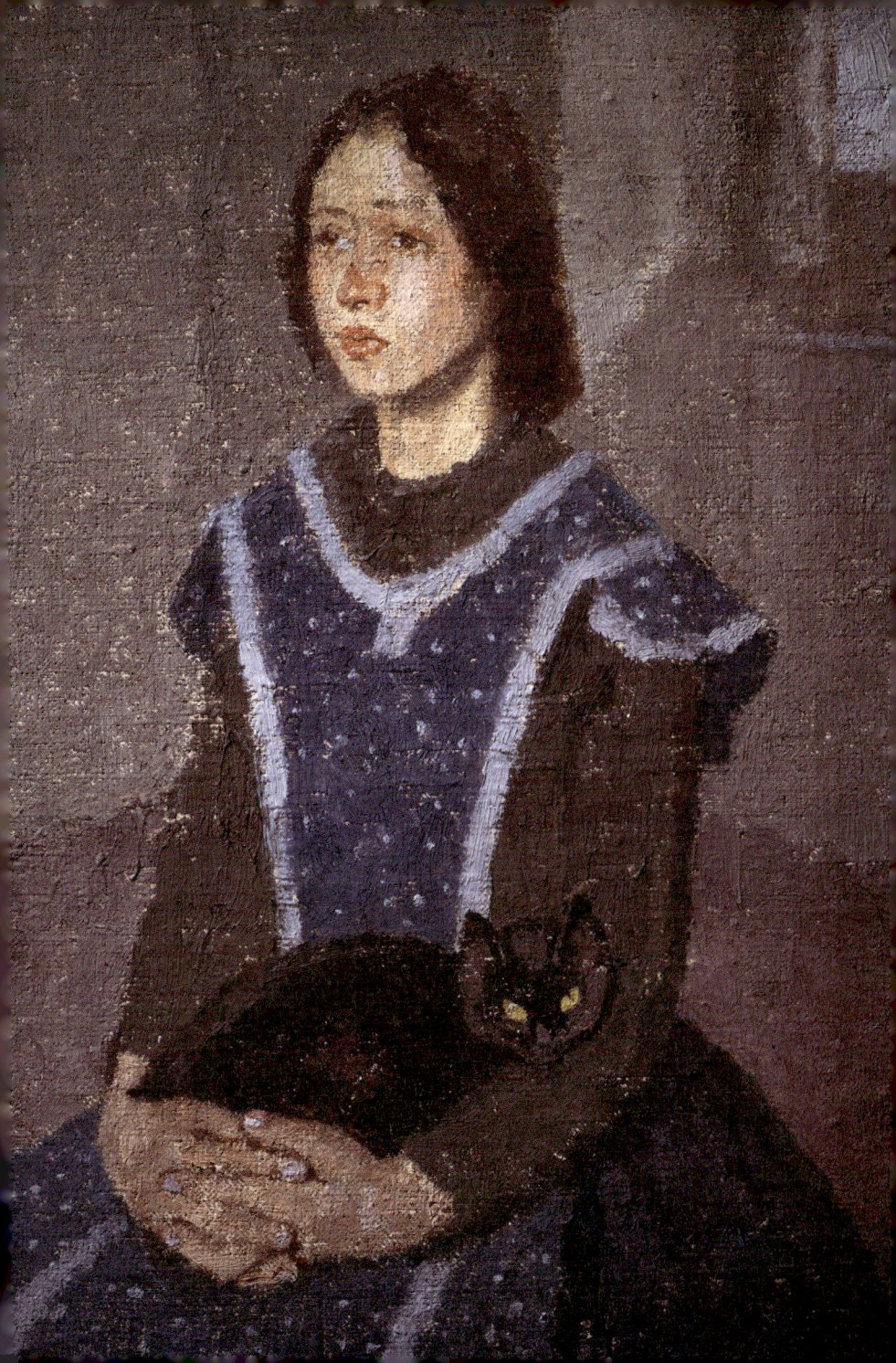

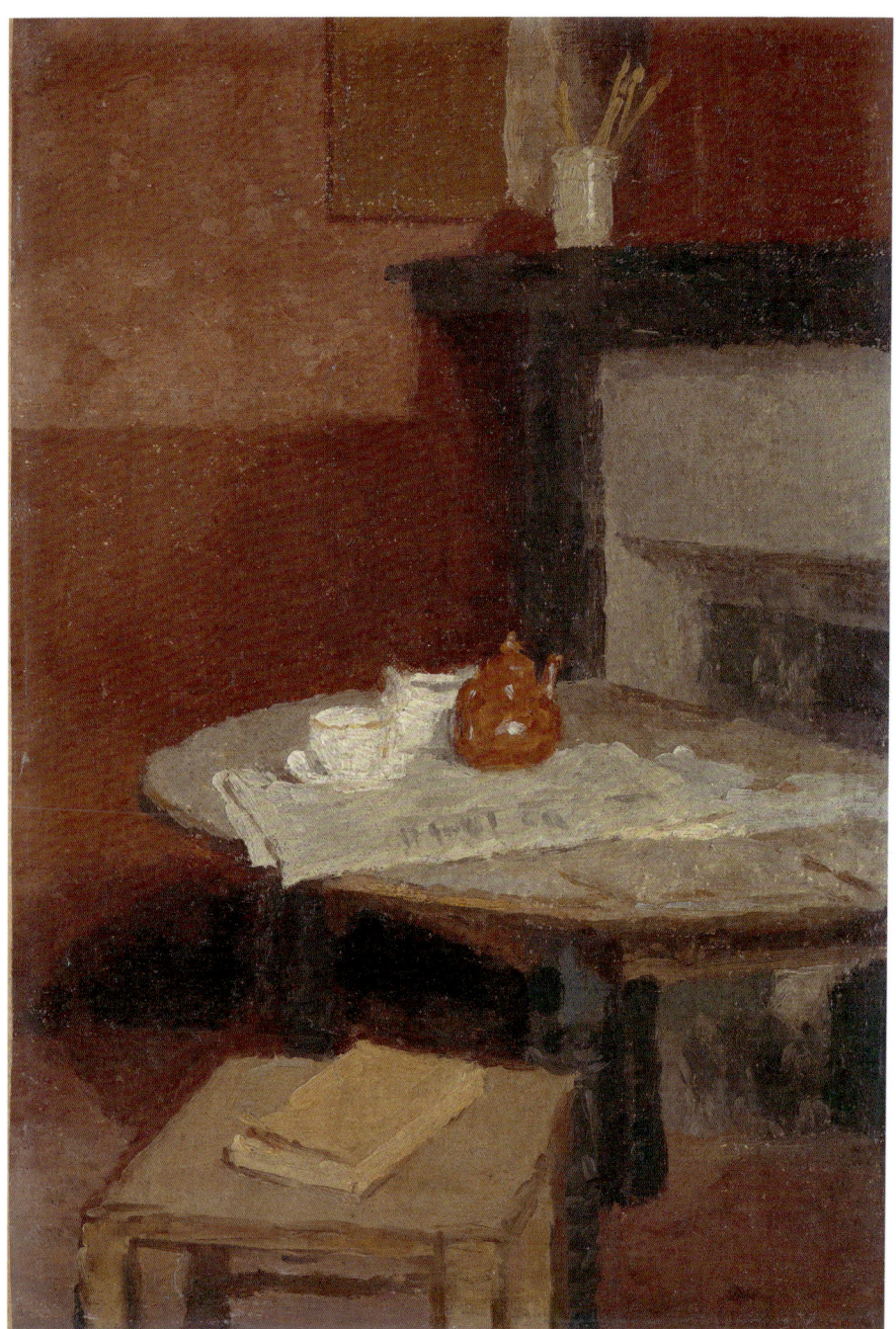

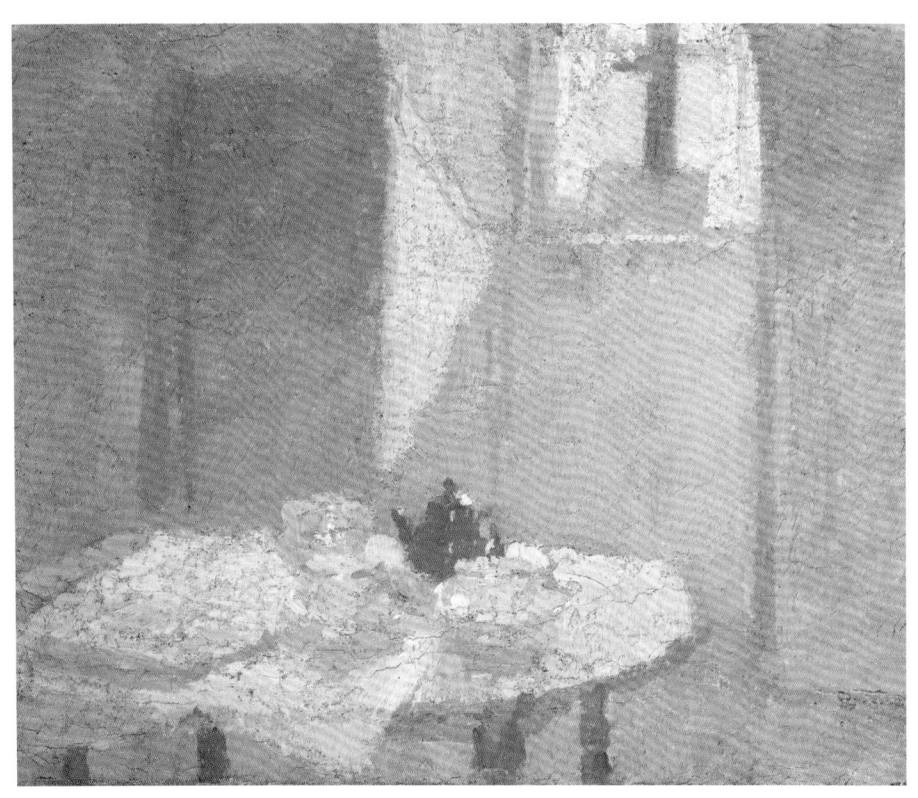

The Brown Teapot c.1915–6
Oil paint on canvas
33.5 × 23.2

Interior c.1924
Oil paint on canvas
22.2 × 27.1

The Japanese Doll 1920s
Oil paint on canvas
33 × 40.6

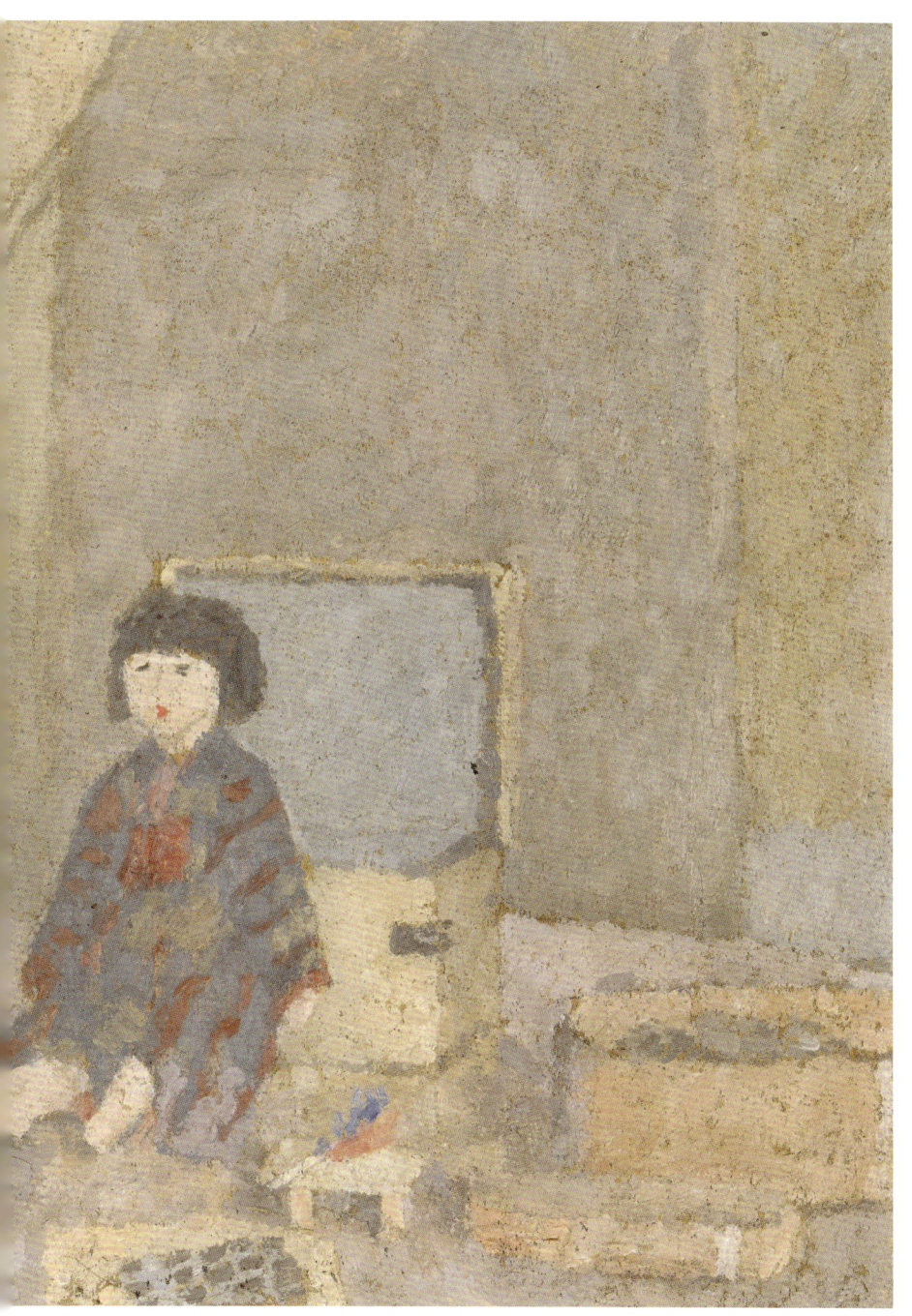

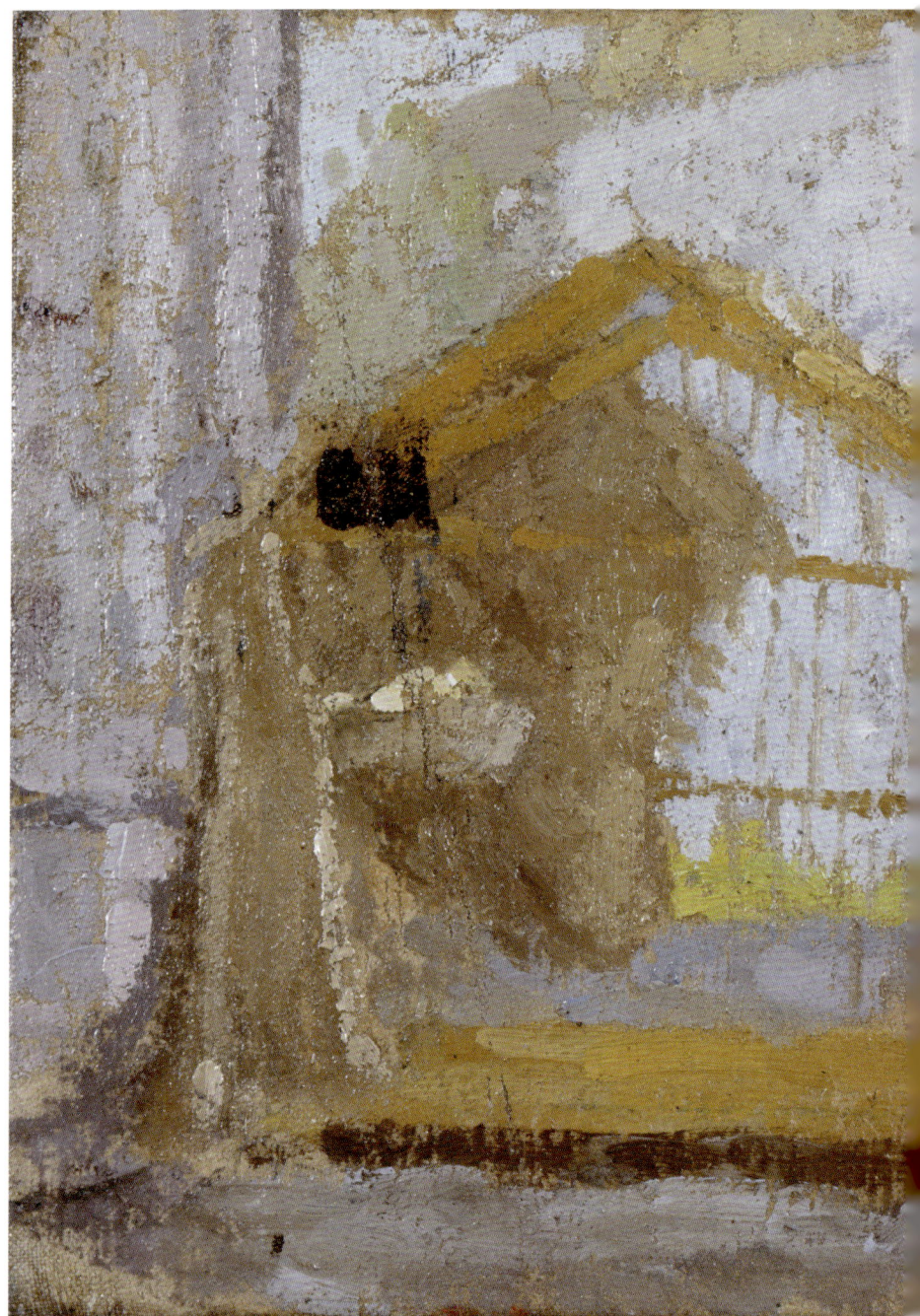

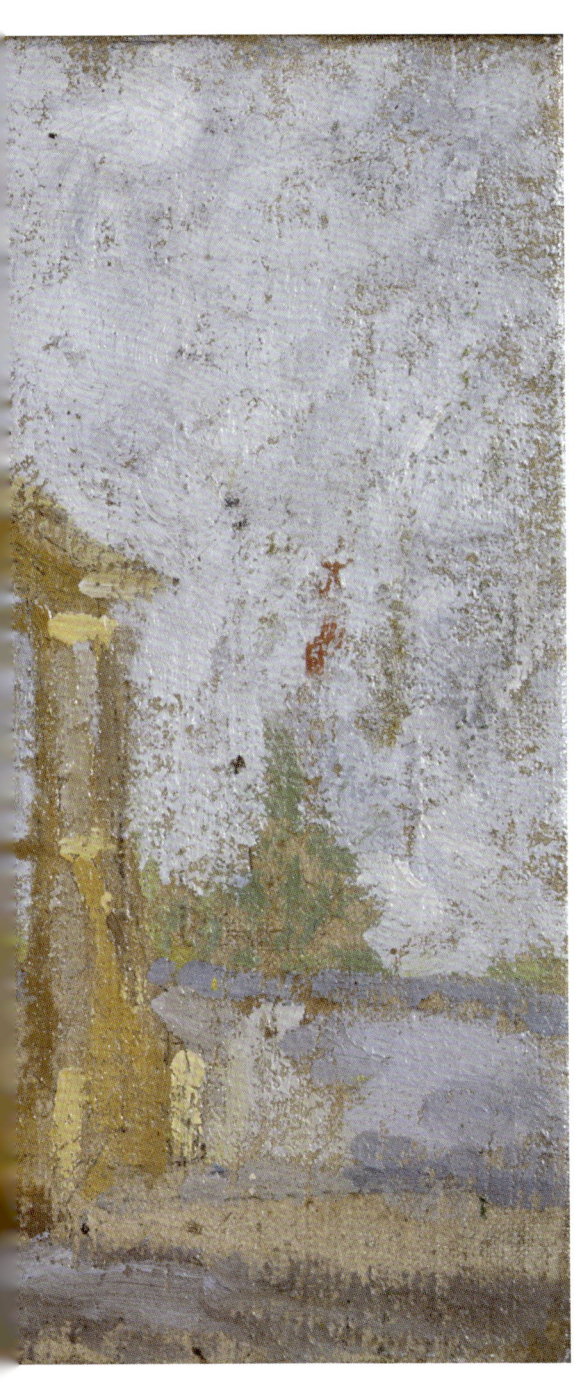

*A Birdcage (House in
a Landscape)* c.1920s
Oil paint on canvas
22.2 × 26.7

Still Life with a Prayer Book,
Shawl, Vase of Flowers and
an Inkwell late 1920s
Oil paint on canvas
26.7 × 21.6

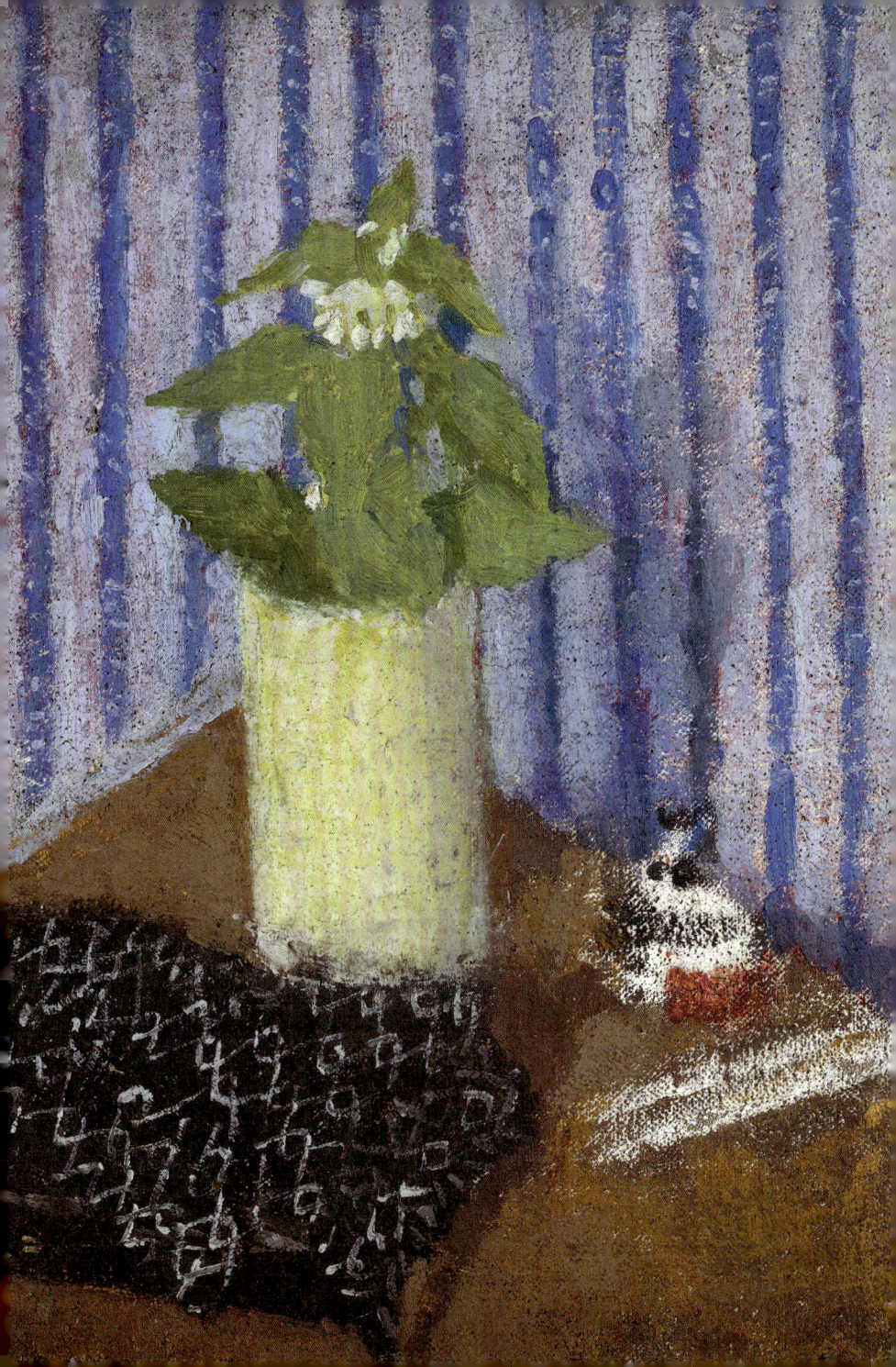

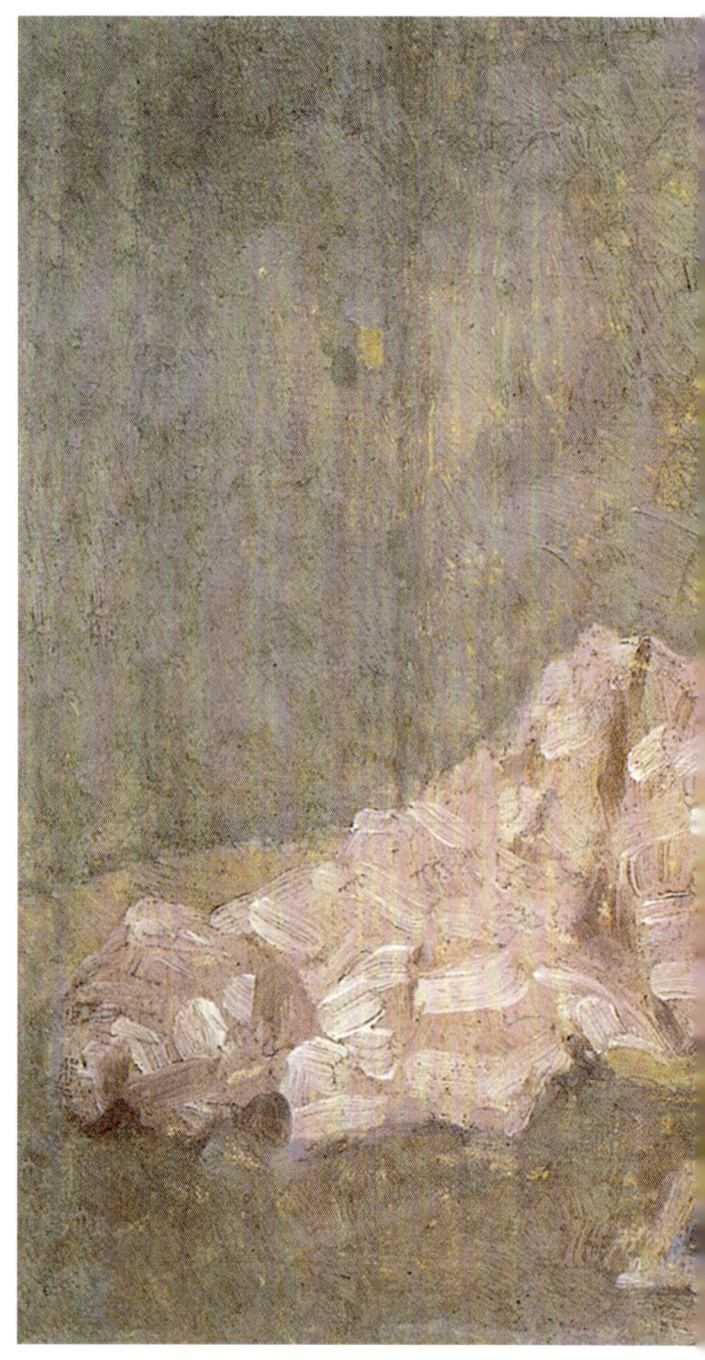

The Straw Hat 1920s
Oil paint on canvas
27 × 33

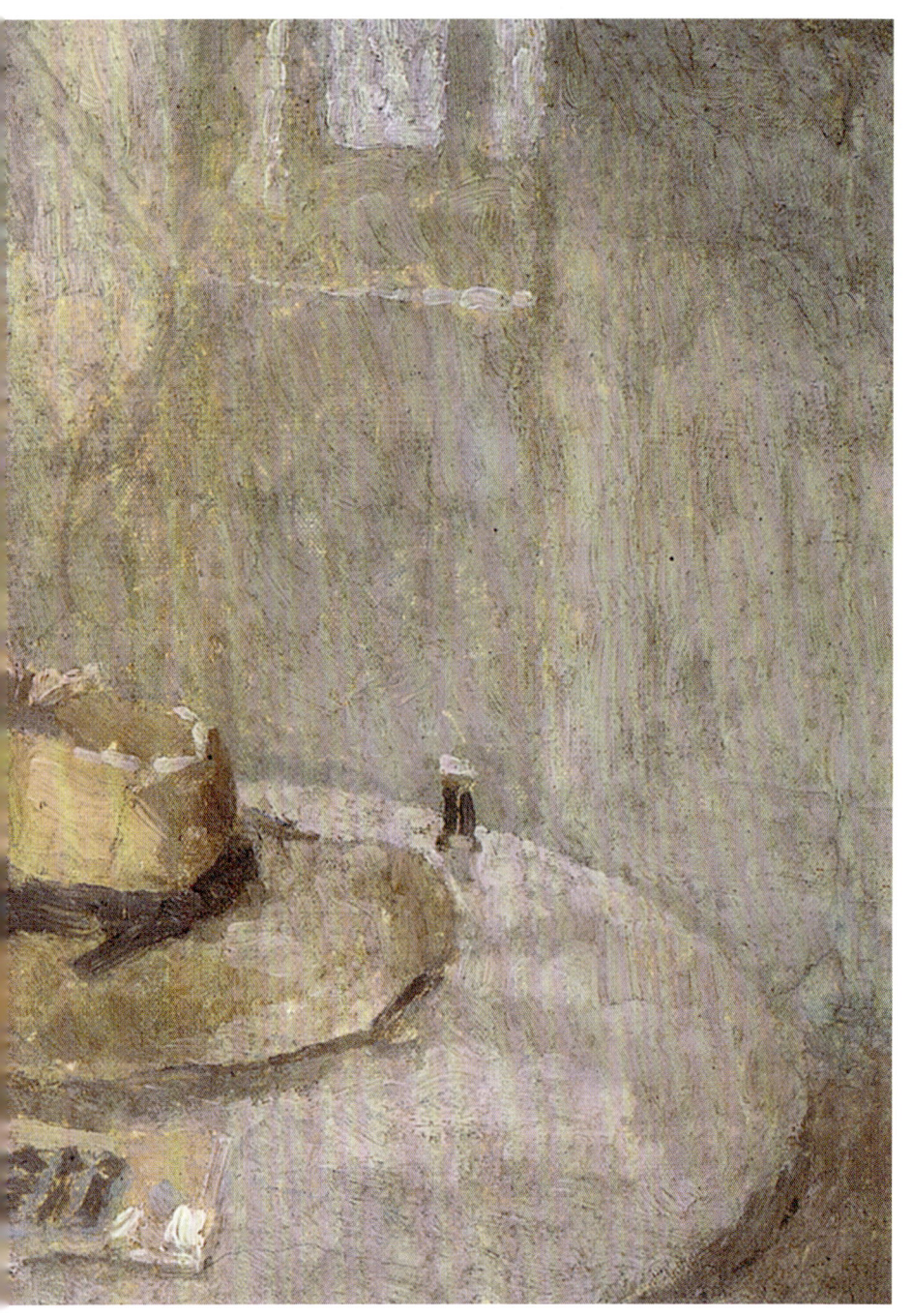

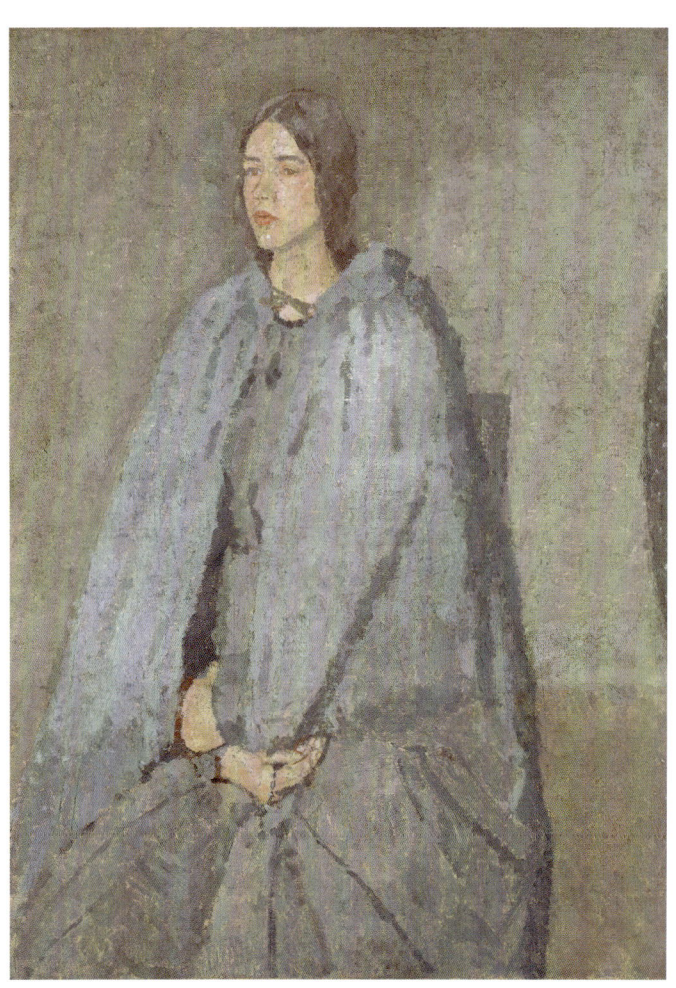

The Pilgrim c.1920
Oil paint on canvas
73.7 × 54.3

Portrait of a Girl in Grey
c.1918–23
Oil paint on canvas
67.3 × 48.3

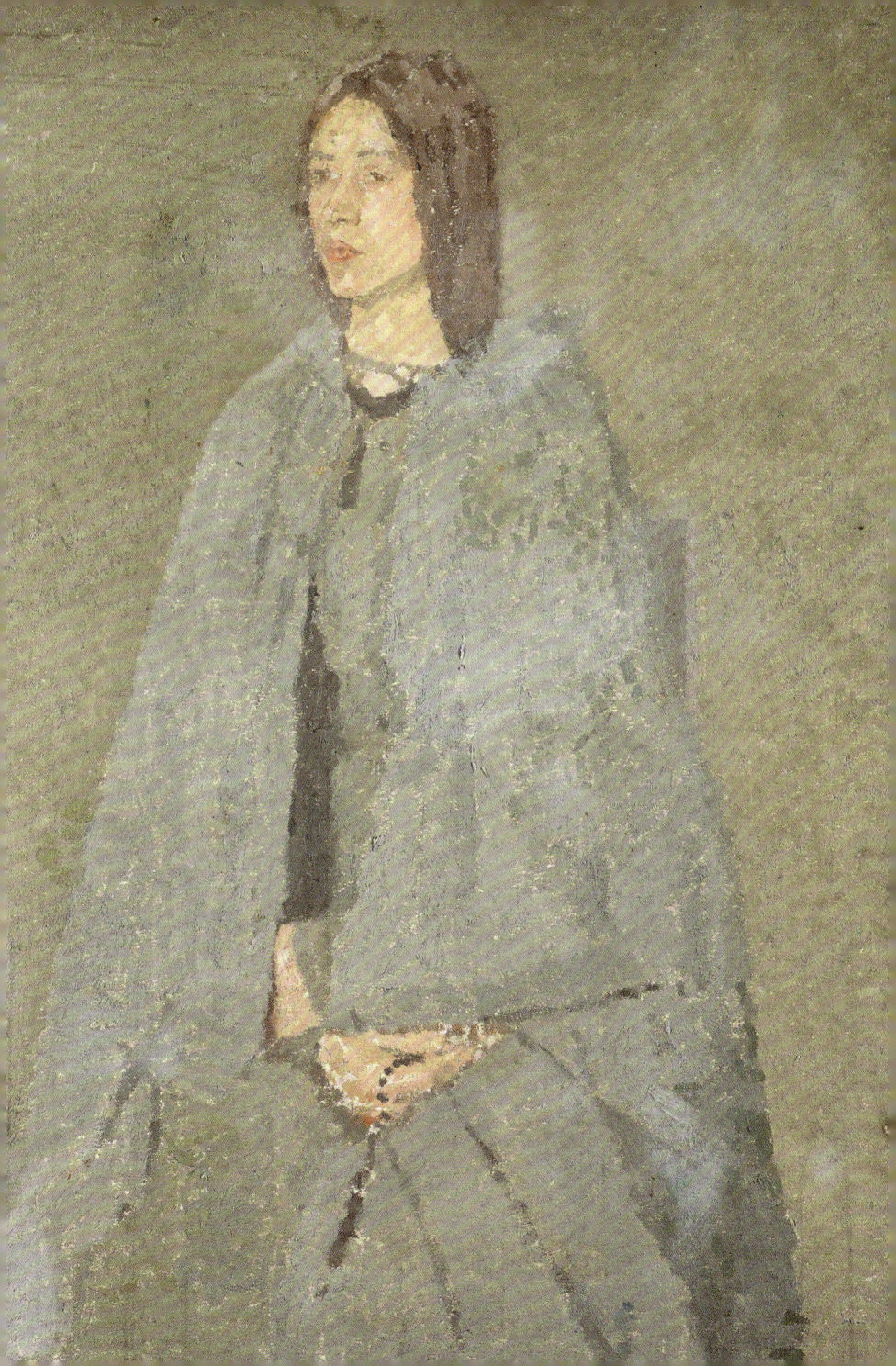

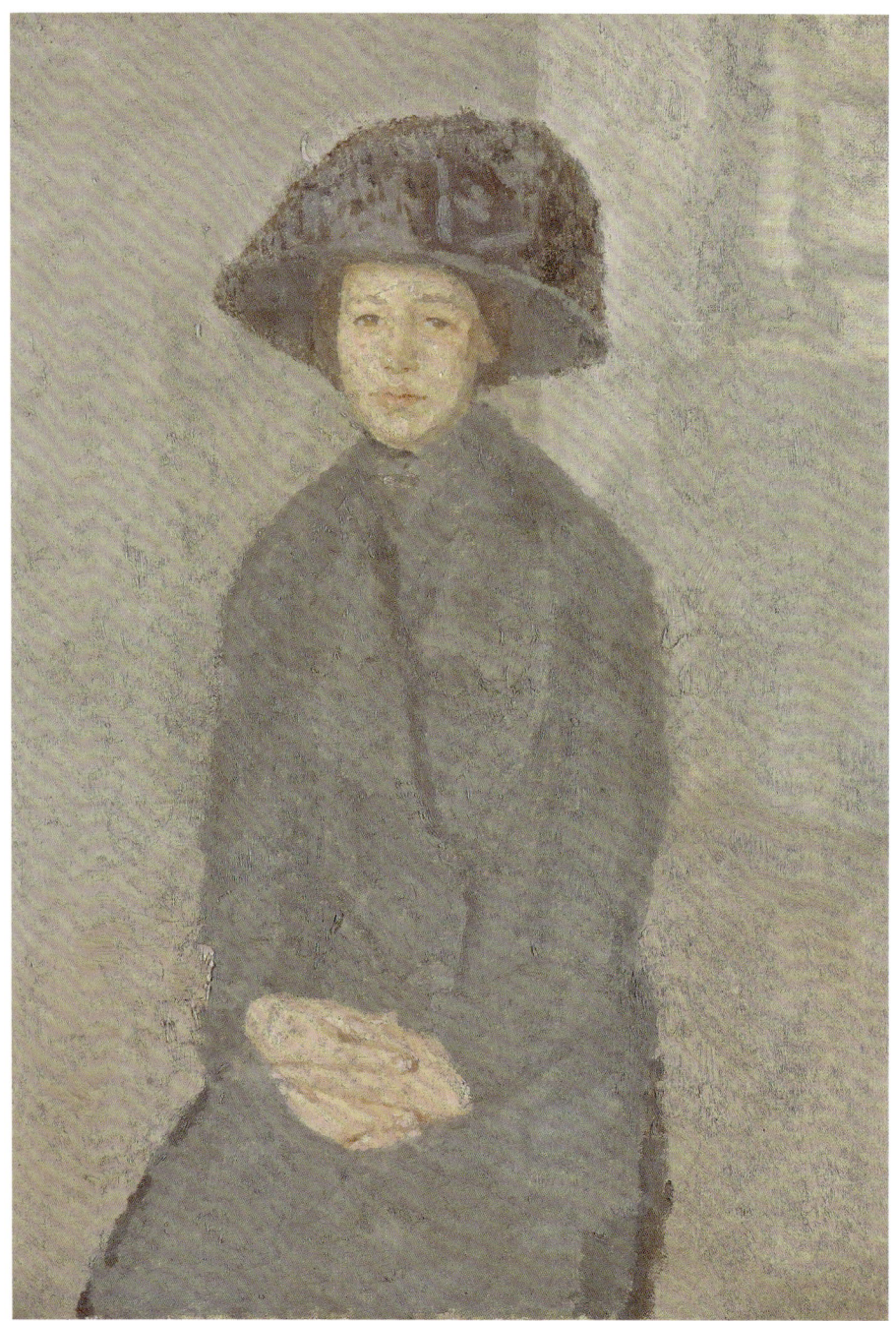

Young Woman c.1920
Oil paint on canvas laid
to panel
47.9 × 36.2

Woman Holding a Flower 1922
Oil paint on canvas
44.7 × 29.2

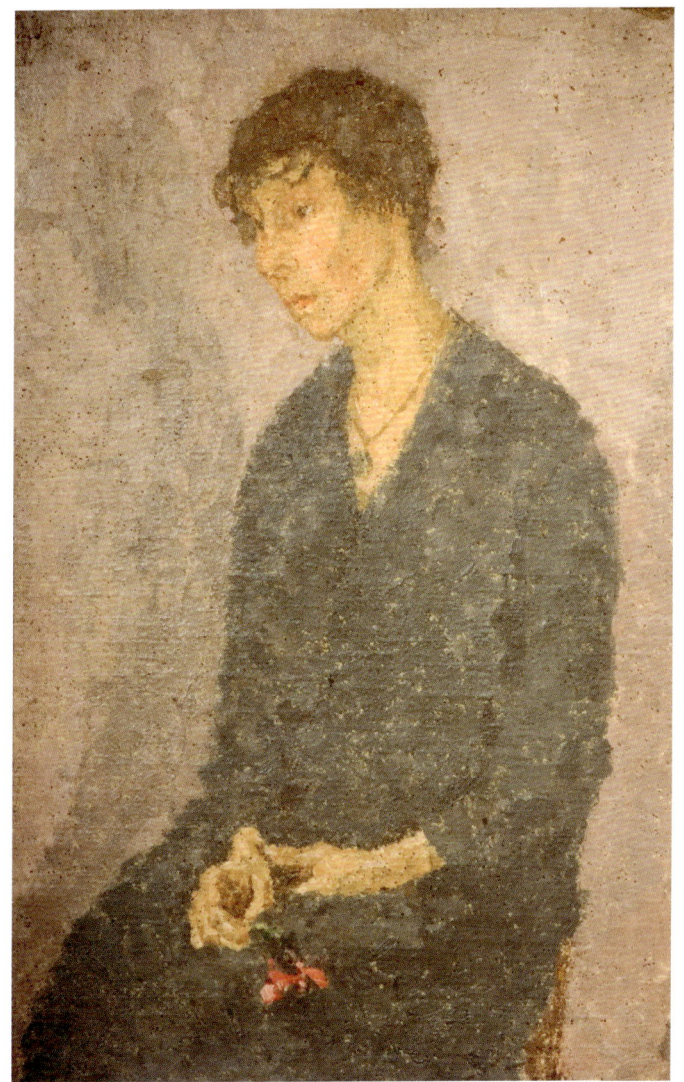

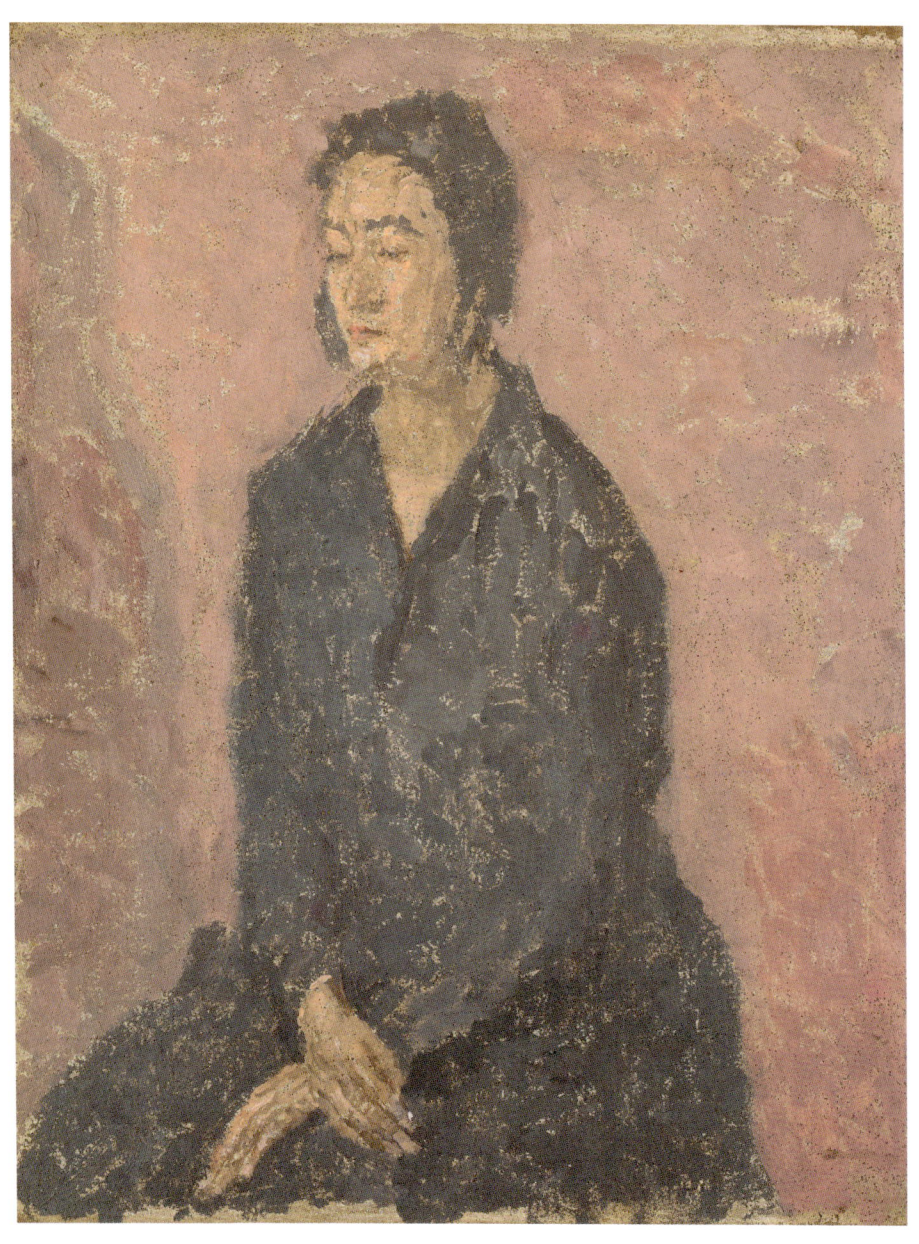

Woman with Hands Crossed
c.1923–4
Oil paint on canvas
40.6 × 33

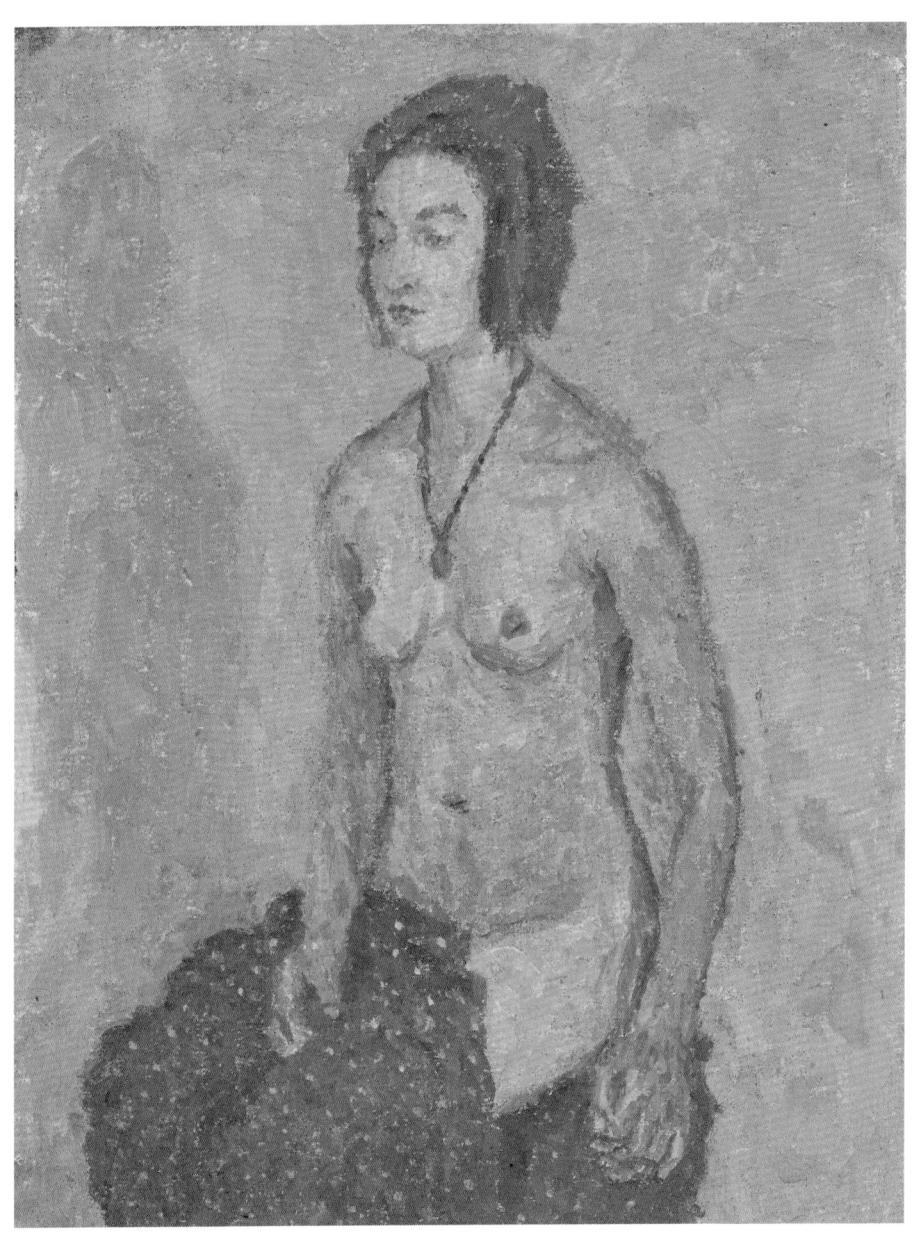

Seated Nude 1923–4
Oil paint on canvas
44.5 × 34.5

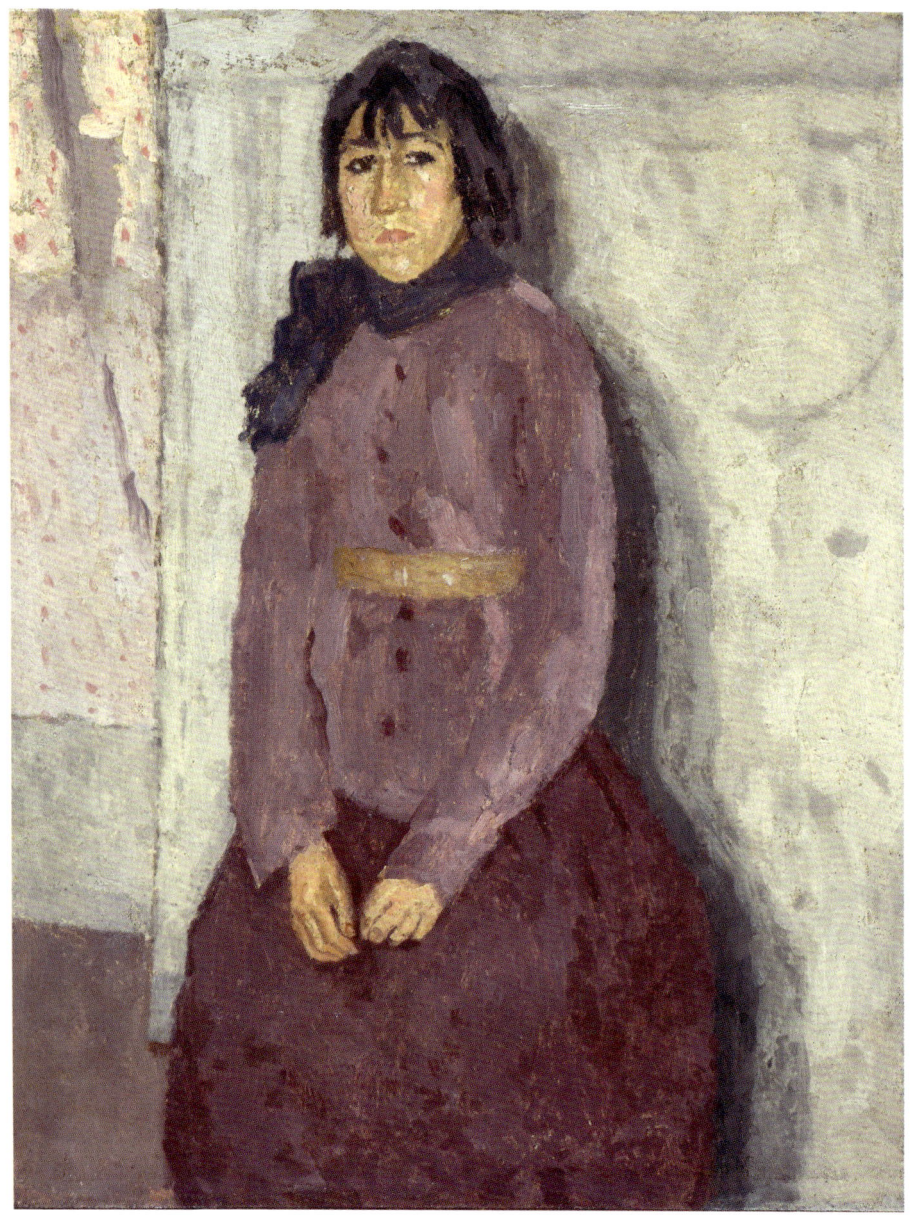

Girl with a Blue Scarf
c.1923–4
Oil paint on canvas
41.1 × 33

Girl in a Mulberry Dress
c.1923–4
Oil paint on canvas
54.6 × 37.5

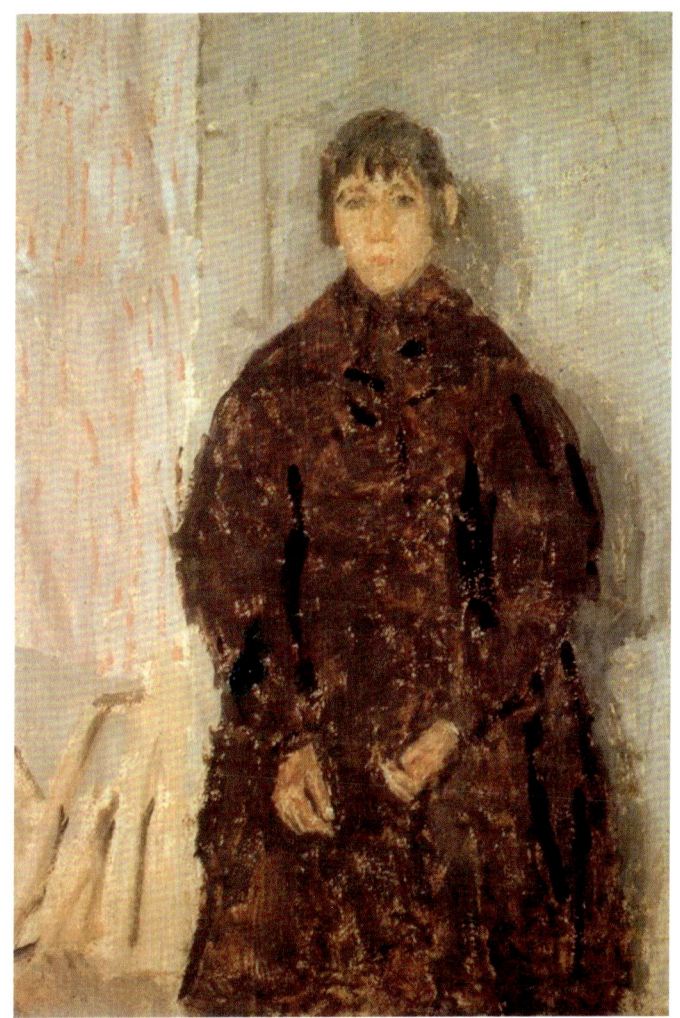

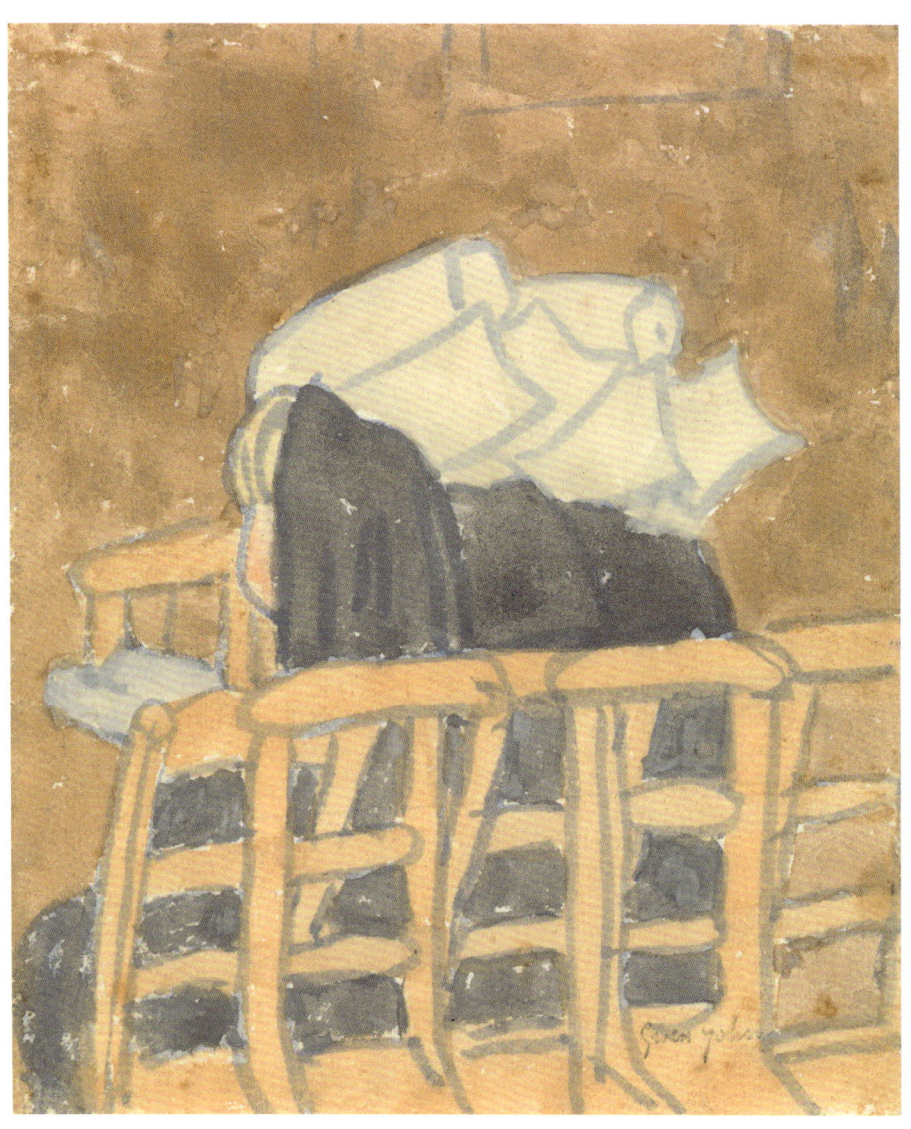

Two Nuns and a Girl in Church
1920s
Watercolour and gouache
on paper
16.5 × 14

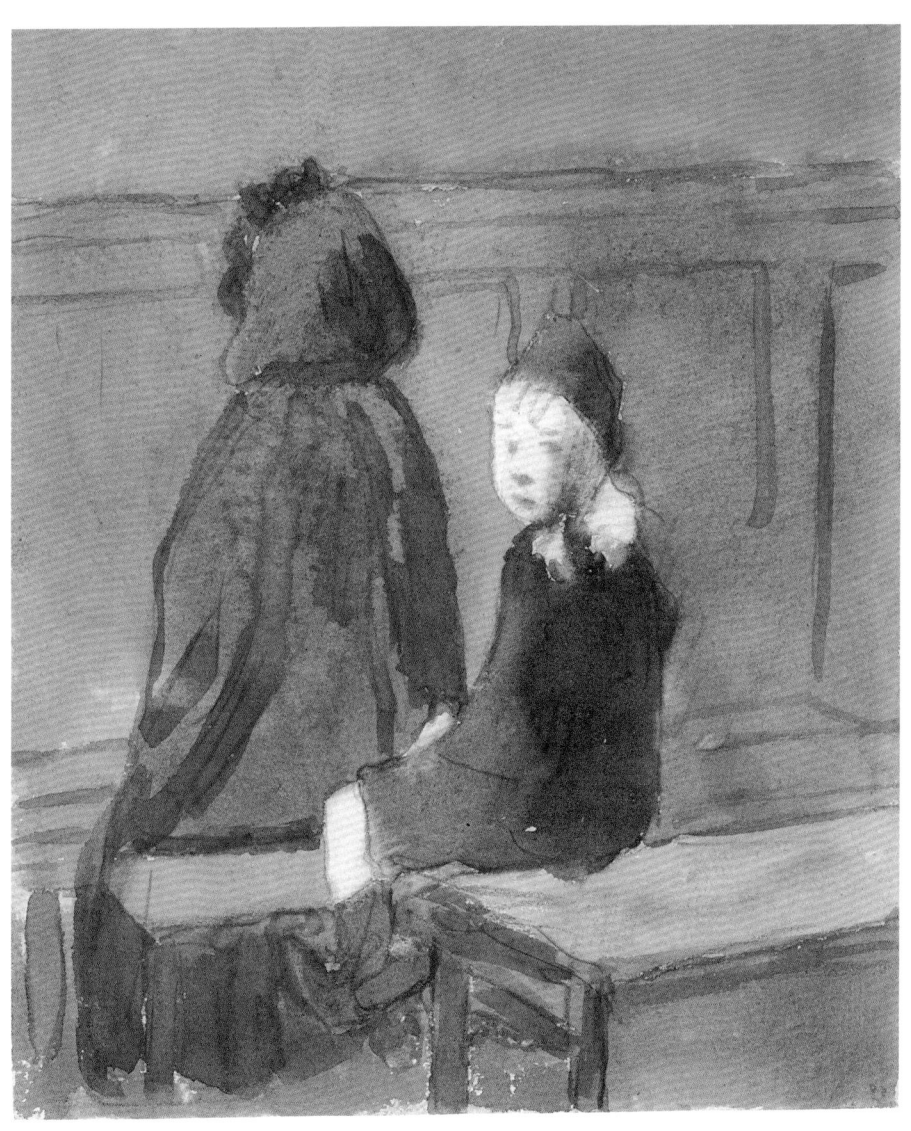

Figures in an Interior
c.1910–20
Graphite and watercolour
on paper
21 × 17.5

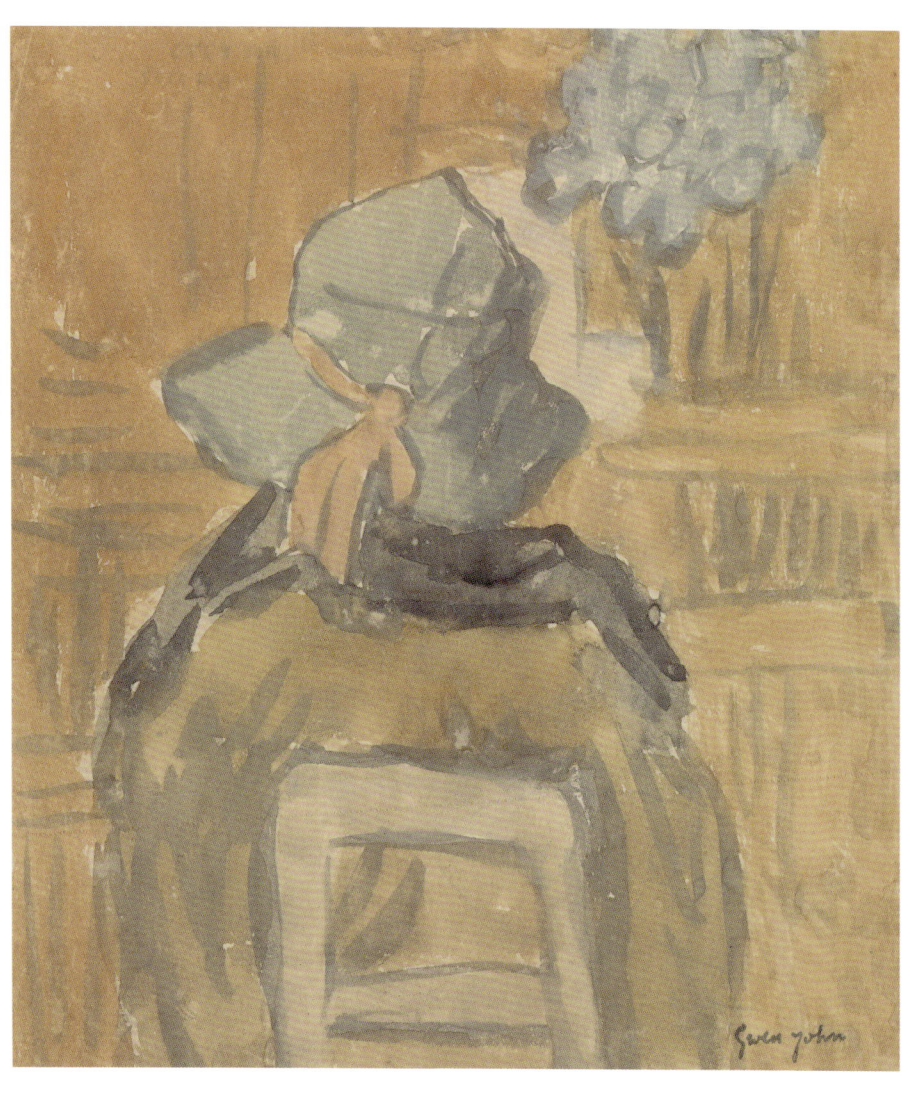

Girl in Church c.1920s
Watercolour on paper
17.1 × 15.2

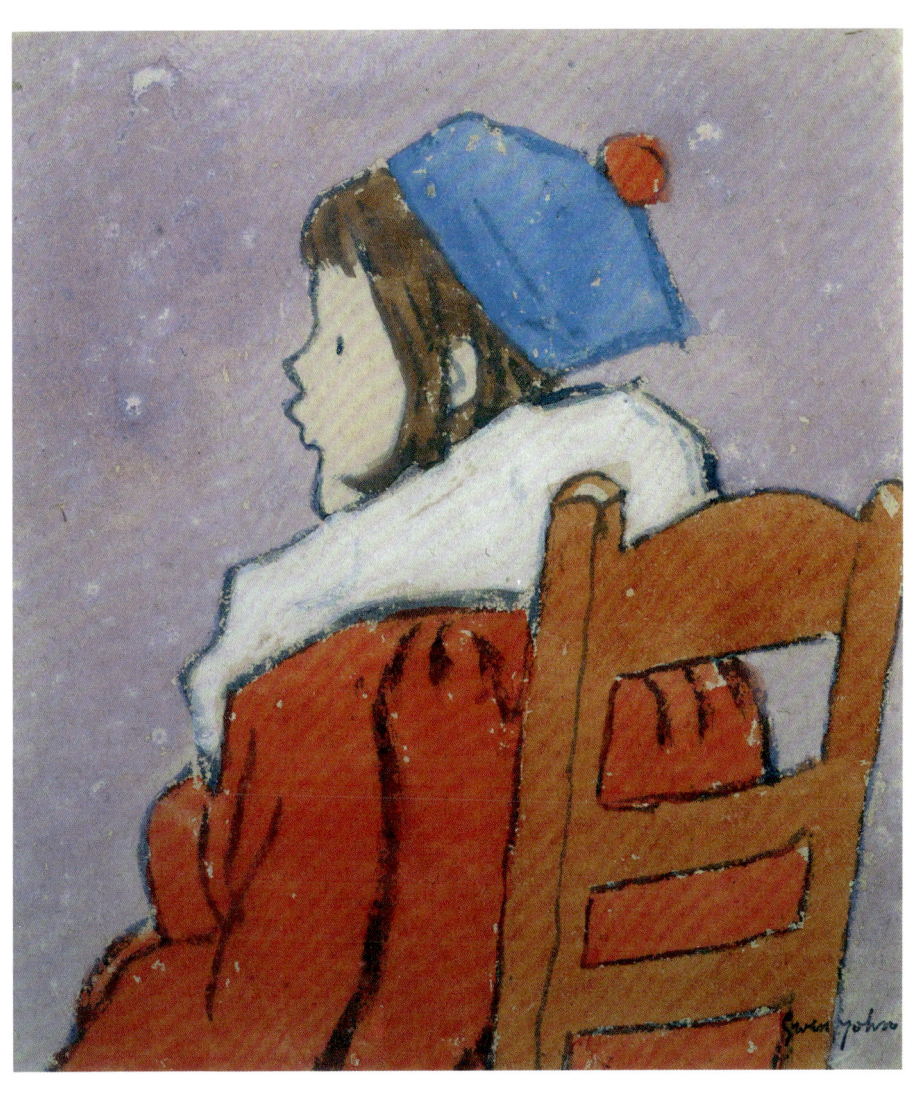

Petit Profil c.1920s
Gouache on paper
16.8 × 15.9

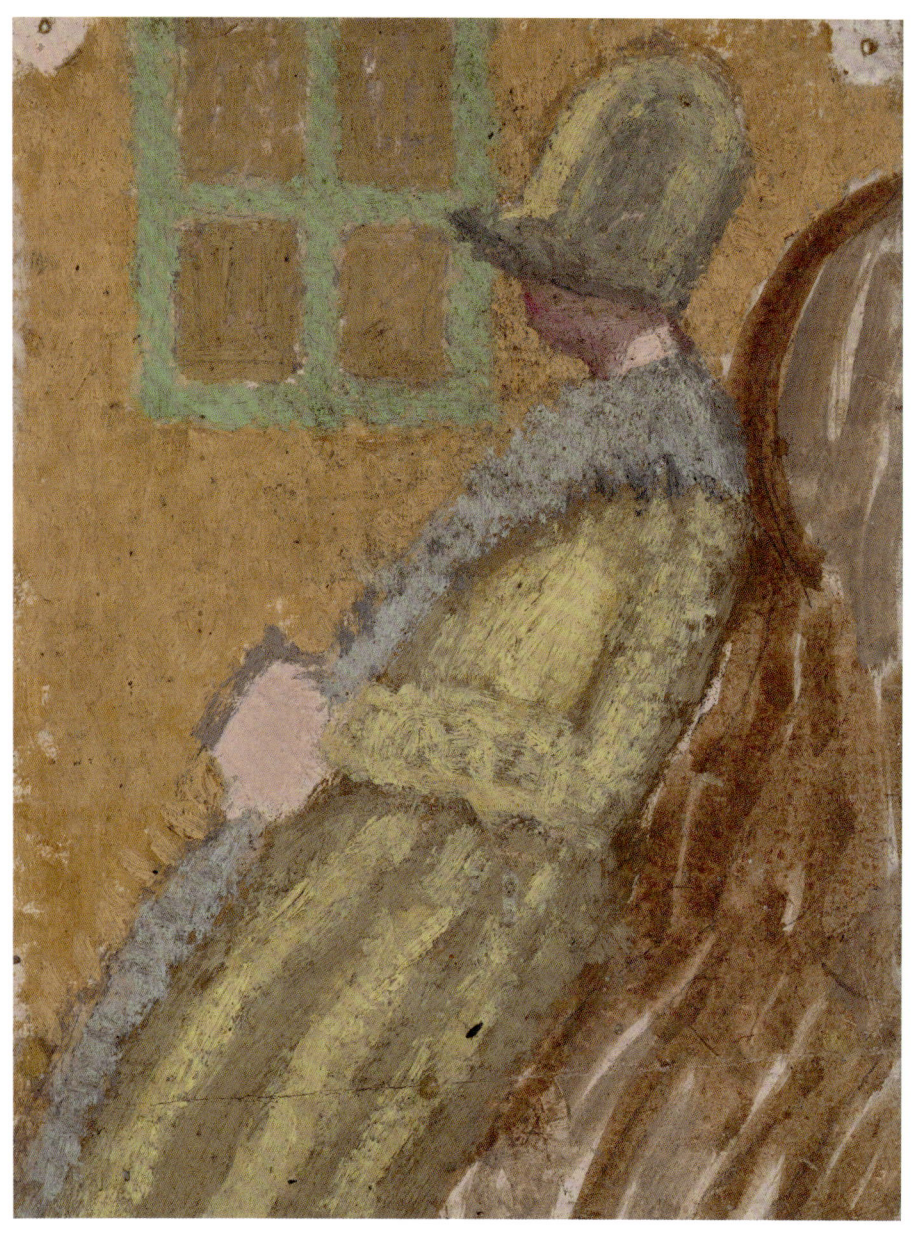

Girl by a Window c.1930s
Oil paint and gouache
on card
16.2 × 12.3

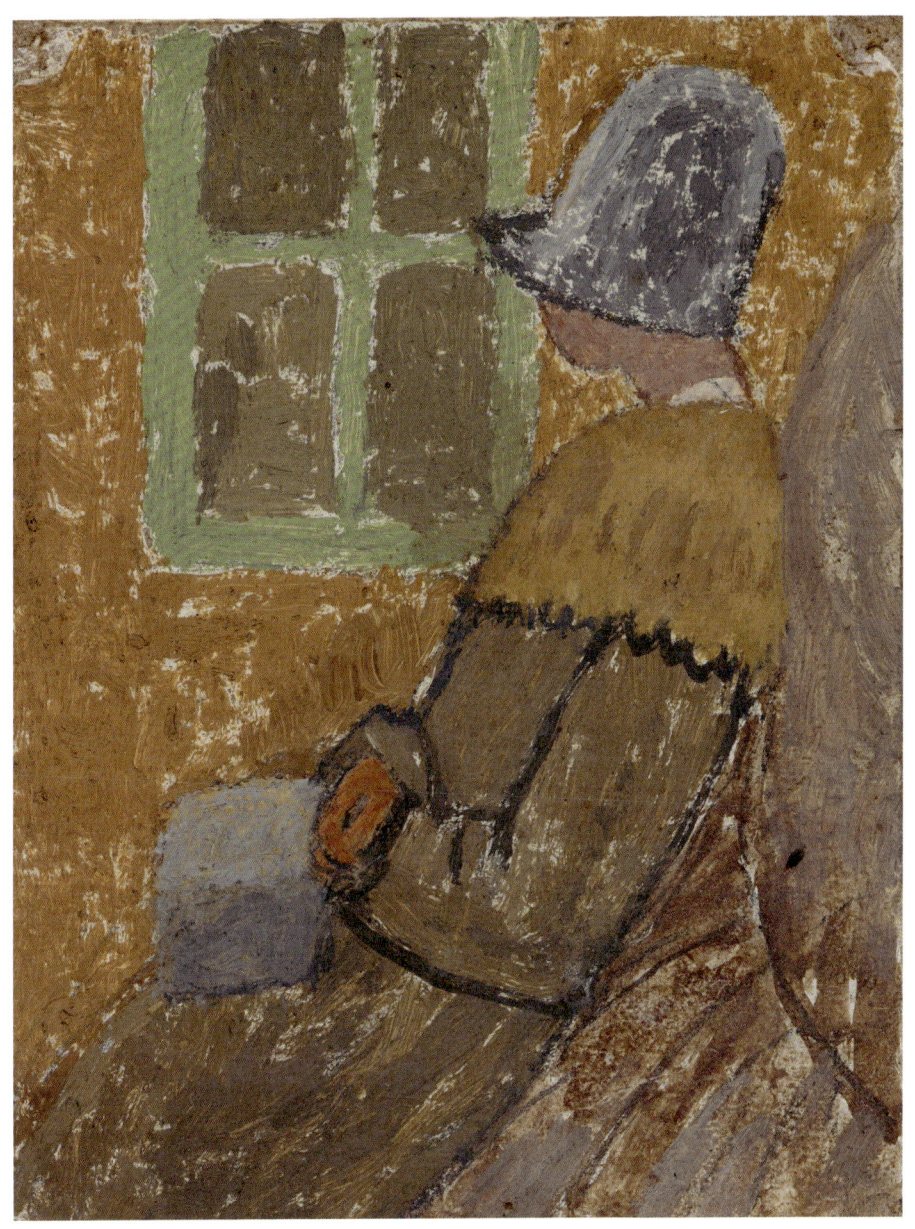

Girl by a Window c.1930s
Oil paint and gouache on
heavy brown paper
16.2 × 12.5

NOTES

1. Jeanne Robert Foster to John Quinn, 16 Sept. 1921, quoted in Cecily Langdale, *Gwen John: With a Catalogue Raisonné of the Paintings*, New Haven and London 1987, p.89.

2. Gwen John to Ursula Tyrwhitt, [?Aug. 1936], in Ceridwen Lloyd-Morgan, *Gwen John: Letters and Notebooks*, London 2004, p.184.

3. See John Rothenstein, 'Gwen John', in *Modern English Painters*, vol.1, London 1952; *Gwen John: An Interior Life*, exh. cat., Barbican Art Gallery, London 1985. For a critique of this characterisation of Gwen John, see Alicia Foster, *Gwen John*, London and Princeton, NJ 1999, pp.6–9, and Alicia Foster, *Gwen John: Art and Life in London and Paris*, London 2023, pp.243–8.

4. Foster 1999, pp.15–16.

5. Ibid., pp.12–14; Foster 2023, p.17.

6. Appearing, for example, on the cover of *Now You See Us: Women Artists in Britain 1520–1920*, exh. cat., Tate Britain, London 2023.

7. Brown's self-portrait was also reproduced in his autobiographical essay 'Recollections', *Artwork*, no.23, 1930, p.151.

8. *Gwen John: An Interior Life*, exh. cat., 1985, pp.28–9; Langdale 1987, pp.1–2; Foster 1999, pp.45–6, 49–50; Foster 2023, pp.214–6, 223–5.

9. John to Ursula Tyrwhitt, 4 Feb. 1910, in Lloyd-Morgan 2004, p.53.

10. Langdale 1987, p.8.

11. Ibid., pp.9, 10.

12. Ibid., p.9.

13. Ida Nettleship to Ada Nettleship, quoted in Michael Holroyd, *Augustus John: A Biography*, revised edn, Harmondsworth 1987, p.113.

14. William Rothenstein, *Men and Memories*, London 1931, vol.2, p.26.

15. Augustus had been obsessed with Dorelia before she and Gwen embarked on their journey to Toulouse. On her return to London, Dorelia entered a *ménage à trois* with him and his wife Ida (Nettleship), whom he had married in 1901. After Ida's early death in 1907, Dorelia became Augustus's lifelong partner. See Holroyd 1987, pp.180–92.

16. Lloyd-Morgan 2004, p.9; Sue Roe, *Gwen John: A Life*, London 2001, p.49.

17. John to Ursula Tyrwhitt, n.d. 1904–5, in Lloyd-Morgan 2004, p.37; Roe 2001, p.53. The *Monument to Whistler* was never finished but a head related to the monument was exhibited in the *Paris Salon* in 1906, and a bronze cast from 1908 and a plaster model for a reworked version 1914–18 are at the Musée Rodin. See Roe 2001, p.80; Foster 2023, pp.75–8.

18. Roe 2001, pp.47–67; Foster 2023, pp.93–6.

19. Langdale 1987, p.44; Foster 2023, pp.80–1.

20. John to Auguste Rodin, quoted in Roe 2001, p.73.

21. Foster 1999, pp.42–3.

22. Roe 2001, p.94.

23. T. Martin Wood, 'The New English Art Club Exhibition' *The Studio*, vol.44, July 1908, pp.138, 141.

24. John to Ursula Tyrwhitt, 15 Oct. [1911], in Lloyd-Morgan 2004, p.70.

25. She wrote to Tyrwhitt: 'The picture I have done for Mr Quinn is the same pose and I have put my own face in and it is more fitting.' Gwen John to Ursula Tyrwhitt, 15 Oct. [1911], in Lloyd-Morgan 2004, p.70.

26. Foster 1999, pp.42–3, 52–5.

27. Foster 2023, p.214.

28. Lovell was also a model for Rodin. See Roe 2001, pp.103, 106; Foster 2023, p.108.

29. Sir John Rothenstein to D.S. MacColl, 21 Dec. 1943, quoted in Mary Chamot, Dennis Farr and Martin Butlin, *The Modern British Paintings, Drawings and Sculpture*, London 1964, vol.2, p.686.

30. Although there is no evidence that the paintings were ever exhibited together, a letter Gwen John wrote to Tyrwhitt implies that she intended to send both works to the NEAC exhibition. In the end, only the clothed version was exhibited. John to Ursula Tyrwhitt, 6 May 1910, in Lloyd-Morgan 2004, p.54.

31. John to Ursula Tyrwhitt, 30 Sept. 1909, in Lloyd-Morgan 2004, p.50.

32. John to John Quinn, 17 Nov. 1912 and 25 Jan. 1913, in Lloyd-Morgan 2004, pp.77–8.

33. Langdale 1987, pp.47–9.

34. Roe 2001, pp.110–11.

35. John to Ursula Tyrwhitt, 3 Aug. 1916, in Lloyd-Morgan 2004 p.96.

36. John to John Quinn, 3 June 1916, in Lloyd-Morgan 2004, p.95; Langdale 1987, p.146.

37. Langdale 1987, p.51.

38. John to Ursula Tyrwhitt, 15 Feb. 1909, in Lloyd-Morgan 2004, p.49.

39. John to Ursula Tyrwhitt, 29 March 1918, in Lloyd-Morgan 2004, p.104.

40. *Gwen John: An Interior Life*, exh. cat., 1985, p.41.

41. Mary Bustin, 'The Rules and Problems of Painting: Gwen John's Later Painting Technique', in David Fraser-Jenkins and Chris Stephens (eds), *Gwen John and Augustus John*, exh. cat., Tate Britain, London, 2004, pp.197–8.

42. Ibid., p.200.

43. Langdale 1987, p.97.

44. Ibid., p.89.

45. Roe 2001, p.185; Langdale 1987, pp.87–8.

46. Langdale 1987, p.88.

47. John to Ursula Tyrwhitt, Aug. 1936, quoted in Langdale 1987, p.97.

48. John to Ursula Tyrwhitt, [?Aug. 1936], in Lloyd-Morgan 2004, p.184.

49. Reproduced in Lloyd-Morgan 2004, p.117.

50. 13 March 1932. Reproduced in Lloyd-Morgan pp.177–8.

51. Roe 2001, pp.202–9, Langdale 1987, p.73.

52. Quinn began sending John an annual stipend in summer 1920. He first arranged to pay $500 yearly for any two paintings and almost immediately raised the stipend to $750 for three paintings. See John Quinn to Gwen John, 14 Aug. 1920 and 29 Aug. 1920, quoted in Langdale 1987, p.73

53. Langdale 1987, p.76; Foster 2023, pp.182–9.

54. John to John Quinn, 15 July 1924, quoted in Langdale 1987, p.76.

55. Quoted in ibid., p.76.

56. Ibid., p.77.

57. Mary Chamot, 'An Undiscovered Artist', *Country Life*, 19 June 1926, pp.884–5.

58. Ibid.

59. Quoted in Langdale 1987, p.80.

60. Ibid., p.81; Foster 2023, pp.195–9.

61. Langdale 1987, p.107.

62. Foster 1999 and Foster 2023 have been particularly important in this respect.

63. John to Ursula Tyrwhitt, 13 Nov. 1908; Lloyd-Morgan 2004, p.48.

CREDITS

© Amgueddfa Cymru - Museum Wales 18, 45, 52, 54, 59, 70–1, 72–3, 90, 91

ARTGEN / Alamy Stock Photo Cover, 13, 33, 37, 43, 65, 85

© Ashmolean Museum, University of Oxford 57

Photo by Birmingham Museums Trust, licensed under CC0 81

Bridgeman Images 58

Photo © Christie's Images / Bridgeman Images 82, 89

Ferens Art Gallery, Hull, UK / Bridgeman Images 7, 61

Photo © Fitzwilliam Museum / Bridgeman Images 62

incamerastock / Alamy Stock Photo 32

© The estate of Augustus John. All Rights Reserved 2020 / Bridgeman Images 37

© Estate of Augustus John. All rights reserved 2024 / Bridgeman Images 10

© Manchester Art Gallery / Bridgeman Images 69

© Manchester Art Gallery / Gift Of Mr Charles Lambert Rutherston, 1925 / Bridgeman Images 63

2024 © Photo Scala, Florence / The Metropolitan Museum of Art / Bequest of Mary Cushing Fosburgh, 1978 (1979.135.27) 34–5 / Bequest of Joan Whitney Payson, 1975 (1976.201.25) 66

2024 © Photo Scala, Florence / The Museum of Modern Art, New York/ Mary Anderson Conroy

Bequest in memory of her mother, Julia Quinn Anderson. Acc. no.: 421.1971. 47 / A. Conger Goodyear Fund. Acc. n.: 124.1958. 49 / Gift of Nelson A. Sears in memory of Mrs. Millicent A. Rogers. Acc. n.: 400.1963. 84

National Galleries of Scotland. Presented by Sir Alexander Maitland in memory of his wife Rosalind, 1960 16

National Galleries of Scotland. Purchased with assistance from the Henry and Sula Walton Fund and Art Fund (with a contribution from the Wolfson Foundation), 2020 79

National Museum of Women in the Arts, Gift of Wallace and Wilhelmina Holladay / Photo by Lee Stalsworth 60

© National Portrait Gallery, London 4

Pallant House Gallery / Justin Piperger 9

The Picture Art Collection / Alamy Stock Photo 44

Private Collection 58

2024 © Photo Scala, Florence / The Metropolitan Museum of Art 34–5, 66

2024 © Photo Scala, Florence / Museum of Modern Art (MoMA) 47, 49 /Gift of Nelson A. Sears in memory of Mrs. Millicent A. Rogers. Acc. n.: 400.1963. 84

Courtesy of Sotheby's 83

Swansea Council: Glynn Vivian Art Gallery Collection 56

Photo: Tate 6, 12, 19, 20, 23, 24, 36, 38, 39, 40–1, 42, 46, 48, 53, 55, 66

© UCL Art Museum, University College London / Bridgeman Images 30–1

Yale Center for British Art, Bequest of Elizabeth S. Tower 86

Yale Center for British Art, Gift of the Libra Foundation, from the family of Nicholas and Susan Pritzker 88

Yale Center for British Art, Paul Mellon Collection 15, 21, 27, 50–1, 68, 74–5, 78, 80, 86, 88

FURTHER READING

Alicia Foster, *Gwen John*, London and Princeton, NJ 1999

Alicia Foster *Gwen John, Art and Life in London and Paris*, London 2023

David Fraser-Jenkins and Cecily Langdale, *Gwen John: An Interior Life*, exh. cat., Barbican Art Gallery, London 1985

David Fraser-Jenkins and Chris Stephens (eds.), *Gwen John and Augustus John*, exh. cat., Tate Britain, London 2004

Cecily Langdale, *Gwen John: With a Catalogue Raisonné of the Paintings*, New Haven and London 1987

Ceridwen Lloyd-Morgan, *Gwen John: Letters and Notebooks*, London 2004

Sue Roe, *Gwen John: A Life*, London 2001

Mary Taubman, *Gwen John*, London 1985

Alison Thomas, *Portraits of women: Gwen John and her forgotten contemporaries*, Cambridge 1994

INDEX

Page references in *italics* indicate images.

First published 2024 by order of the Tate Trustees
by Tate Publishing, a division of Tate Enterprises Ltd
Millbank, London SW1P 4RG
www.tate.org.uk/publishing

© Tate Enterprises Ltd 2024

Emma Chambers has asserted her right under the
Copyright, Designs and Patents Act, 1988, to be
identified as Author of this Work

Text © Emma Chambers

All rights reserved. No part of this book may be
reprinted or reproduced or utilised in any form
or by any electronic, mechanical or other means,
now known or hereafter invented, including
photocopying and recording, or in any information
storage or retrieval system, without permission in
writing from the publishers or a licence from the
Copyright Licensing Agency Ltd, www.cla.co.uk

A catalogue record for this book is available from
the British Library

ISBN 978 1 84976 951 8

Distributed in the United States and Canada by
ABRAMS, New York

Library of Congress Control Number applied for

Commissioning Editor: Emma Poulter
Editorial Assistant: Aki Gurung
Production: Juliette Dupire
Picture Researcher: Sarah Tucker
Designed by Astrid Stavro Studio
Colour reproduction by DL Imaging, London
Printed and bound in Italy by Printer Trento, S.r.l

Cover: *Chloë Boughton-Leigh* 1910 (detail, see p.43)
Frontispiece: *Autoportrait à la Lettre* c.1907–9
(detail, see p.37)

Measurements of artworks are given in
centimetres, height before width and depth

THE AUTHOR
Emma Chambers is Curator, Modern British Art
at Tate.

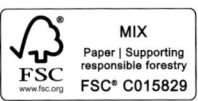

MIX
Paper | Supporting
responsible forestry
FSC® C015829
FSC www.fsc.org